Miracles happen

> But seek first the kingdom of God and His righteousness, and all these things shall be added to you.
> Matthew 6:33

All Bible references are from
The New International Version
unless otherwise stated

First published in 2006
Copyright © 2006

All rights reserved.
No part of this publication may be
reproduced in any form without
prior permission from the publisher.
British Library Cataloguing in Publication Data.
A catalogue record for this book is available
from the British Library.

ISBN 1 903921 37 6

Published by
AUTUMN HOUSE
Grantham, England.

Printed in Thailand

Miracles happen

A GUIDE TO HEALING THE NEW TESTAMENT WAY

David Collinson

Foreword
A Ministry of Healing in the 21st Century
by Rob Frost, Share Jesus International

David Collinson's book makes an important contribution to the Christian apologetic for the healing ministry. It comes at a time when there is an increased interest in healing and the initial stirrings of a rediscovery of the power of Christ to heal within the established churches.

In some contemporary ministerial training the authority of the Bible is questioned and the miracles of Christ are refuted. This kind of outmoded teaching stems from a form of Christian existentialism which denies the supernatural as a reality. Student ministers and church leaders are taught to revere the German Lutheran theologian Rudolf Bultmann, who denied the objective reality of Jesus' healings. Sadly, the influence of scholars such as these on generations of Christian ministers has largely eradicated the church's healing ministry.

It's little wonder, then, that Geddes and Grosset, in their *Guide to Natural Healing* could say of the church: 'The only form of healing accepted by many churches is so-called "spiritual" healing. If genuine physical healing takes place, it is regarded as a problem; the Catholic church tends to distance itself from healers who claim divine inspiration in case these healers should turn out to be charlatans. While this approach is no doubt politic, it tends to undermine the place of healing in religious life. As well as this many Christians believe that the "well of healing" dried up with the early church and limit the healing ministry of Christ to three short years of his life.'

The leaders of some denominations seem to show more interest in disputing the historical truth of the miracles than in recognising their potential for inspiring us to heal today. I've heard sermons in which healing miracles are interpreted as having only a symbolic message for us, and in which contemporary healing miracles are considered to be an embarrassment!

At the beginning of his public ministry Jesus announced that the Kingdom of God was near (Mark 1:15) and immediately he began to heal the sick and to cast out demons. Of the 3,774 verses in the four gospels 484 relate specifically to the healing of physical and mental illness and to the resurrection of the dead.

Jesus commissioned his seventy-two disciples to heal the sick and he assured them that the Kingdom of God was near (Luke 10:9, 10). He promised everyone who believed in him that they could perform the same miracles that he did (John 14:12). One of the signs of the believing church was that they would lay their hands on the sick and see them recover (Mark 16:16-18).

These healing miracles did not end with the ascension, however. Peter, in the first miracle after Pentecost, gave strength to a man who was born 'lame'. Paul healed a man who had been 'lame from birth' at Lystra. When Eutychus fell from the third storey of a building and was 'taken up dead', Paul restored him to life again. Paul is credited with healing many of the people of Malta.

It's time for contemporary Christians to rediscover their own ministry of healing. We need to quote James 5:14-16 to our congregations; and encourage them to do the business which rightly belongs to us!

'Is any sick among you? Let him call for the elders of the church; and let them pray over him, anointing him with oil in the name of the Lord: And the prayer of faith shall save the sick, and the Lord shall raise him up; and if he have committed sins, they shall be forgiven him.'

For too long we have practised the laying off of hands. The Christian healing ministry has been discarded, or left to 'experts' in the life of the church. I have come to believe that every Christian should pray for the gift of healing, and that all of us should practise the 'laying on of hands' for the sick as part of our everyday commitment to Jesus Christ.

I'm deeply aware that I have no personal healing power, and have no 'heat-transmitting' gift or scientific understanding of human disease. I do have faith in Jesus Christ, however, and I do believe that his power is available and powerful. When I lay hands on someone in need I am doing it in his name and for his glory. Representing him to a needy and broken world.

During the writing of this book one of my friends came close to death no fewer than four times during a traumatic time in hospital. As I paced the hospital corridor in the early hours of a dark Sunday morning I overheard two doctors discussing the prognosis. They doubted whether he would survive 'till morning, and I was summoned to bring his next of kin.

I have no doubt that what happened during the hours of that night was a healing miracle. I am convinced that Jesus Christ intervened and overruled. I saw it with my own eyes and I believe it with all my heart.

If David's book encourages Christian leaders to engage on a rediscovery of the Christian healing ministry, it will have done a significant job for the extension of God's Kingdom.

About the author

Born in Newcastle upon Tyne during World War Two, David Collinson has worked as a pastor since 1968, serving churches in England and Scotland. He has held a number of hospital chaplaincy posts, holds Masters' degrees in Theology from the Universities of Cambridge and Aberdeen, and a degree in General Studies from Durham University. He has written a number of books and articles, mostly on Healing and Pastoral Studies.

He lives in Northumberland with his wife Anne, and has two daughters and a son, now grown up.

He currently devotes all his time to writing and teaching the Christian faith. His many interests include music and mountains, but his chief passion is to communicate his faith to people in terms that they will understand.

Author's preface

Welcome to this guide. It is a book for everyone, on a subject relevant to everyone, but if it does have a particular target, it is the person seeking a life of meaning, inner peace and stability in a world teeming with options and uncertainties, and who is checking out Christianity to see if it can deliver. So it starts where people are, not where I think they should be; and because many people are not in the position of believing that 'the Bible is true', it assumes that its readers will need to be shown evidence that we can rely on the Bible stories that it 'visits'.

Like every book, it has both limitations and limits. Its limitations are that while it seeks to answer many of its readers' questions concerning healing, it doesn't have all the answers, just enough answers to be going on with. Its limits are that it is a pastoral book, focusing on the needs of the individual. Of course, relationships can also need healing, and so can communities, whole societies, the land, or the planet itself. Christianity is concerned with all these things; but this book concerns itself with the healing of individuals, albeit in the hope that individuals can be set free to bring about healing in the wider world.

The material in the book has various sources. Much of it stems from my reflections on thirty-seven years of pastoral work in the light of the Scriptures. But there has also been a great deal of research, begun at the University of Aberdeen in the early 1990s, and continued thereafter. The research programme involved searching the Scriptures and their background, interviewing many practitioners of healing, and visiting various healing centres, sometimes sharing in their ministry. I learnt much from those visits, which has found its way into this volume, and am profoundly grateful for the experience.

My thanks are due to Dr Rex Gardiner of Sunderland, who first suggested publishing the material, and to Professors Alan Main and Howard Marshall, who supervised the research and were a great source of encouragement. Also, much loving thanks is due to my long-suffering wife Anne, who often helped when computers baffled or infuriated me.

Table of Contents

section 1 — 9
Getting there
- The Territory
- The approach route: The Old Testament
- Obstacles to entry
- Equipment necessary

section 2 — 32
A tour of the healing stories in the Gospels

section 3 — 101
A tour of the healing stories in Acts

section 4 — 129
A tour of other important passages

section 5 — 171
Where do we go from here?
- What must we do?
- What must we believe?

APPENDIX — 182
Other Gospel Passages on Healing

Bibliography — 185

Boxed Byways:
Differences between the Gospels	43
Demons and Deliverance	50
Doctor Luke	69
Health in John's Gospel	80
Words and Things	106
Magic and Miracle	112
Objects, Substances, Shrines and Sacrament	142
The Holy Spirit's Work	153

section 1

Getting there

The Territory

A university don once told me that only someone with a third-rate brain begins a piece of writing by defining his terms. Nevertheless it is important at the beginning to define some terms, and leave readers to draw whatever conclusions they wish about the author's intelligence.

Medical people do not use the term 'healing' very much, and when they do it is usually in the sense: 'that fracture (or that ulcer) has healed'. In popular parlance, the term tends to mean a form of therapy other than normal medicine. In this book we shall take it as meaning the restoration of people to emotional, mental or physical health through prayer, the Christian sacraments and the gifts of the Holy Spirit. Irenaeus, one of the great theologians of the Early Christian Church, wrote that 'the glory of God is a human being fully alive': a wonderful remark which makes one want to call out, 'Yes!' Healing is the process of helping someone to become such a person.

This book is meant to resemble a travel guide. A travel guide usually begins by giving the reader an overview of the territory it will be describing. If we liken healing to a country, it has to be said that there are border disputes. Some Christians would dispute whether healing belongs to the Church at all, and think that it should be occupied entirely by medicine. Other, rather extreme, Christians hold the opposite view and say that such is the power of God that people of faith do not need medicine. In other words, for them the territory belongs to the Church and the practitioners of its ministry of healing. Most Christians, however, are more or less wise and balanced, and think that the territory should be jointly occupied.

Healing also has rather vague boundaries. For some people 'healing', 'holiness' (i.e. serious goodness and spirituality), and 'salvation' (i.e. forgiveness for the wrongdoing in one's life, acceptance by God and the assurance of going to heaven), are separate territories, adjacent to one another it is true, but different. For others, however, they are alternative names for the same territory.

For me, two things are certain:

Firstly, these concepts, healing, salvation, holiness, etc, are rather like tractors and trailers in the road haulage industry. The tractor and trailer are different entities, and have to be distinguished from each other, but they are nevertheless a unity, always work together, and neither is much use without the other!

Secondly, 'healing', 'holiness', and 'salvation'," along with other terms like 'wholeness' or 'life more abundant', wherever you place their boundaries, are all just parts of a much bigger thing called 'The Kingdom of God'.

The approach route: The Old Testament

The Old Testament is vast, but no one can ignore it if he wants to understand the teaching on healing contained in the New.

In this book we are, as it were, overflying the Old Testament to land in the middle of the New, but we can justify this short cut if we make the flight into a reconnaissance, taking careful note of the main features of the landscape of the Old Testament on the way.

Picture a dignified gentleman of biblical times. He is somewhat advanced in years but is in possession of all his faculties, has the strength of someone far younger and is in perfect health. He lives in a time of peace, and lives at peace with his immediate neighbours. He is prosperous, has 'exceeding many' flocks and herds, oxen and asses. Beautiful and super-competent wives have borne him many sons and a few daughters too. When he takes his seat at the town gate he is received and listened to with respect, because he is genuinely caring and wise: a man, in fact, at peace with himself, his friends and neighbours, and, above all, with God. And he is like this because he is caring and good, and concerned to obey all God's commands: that is to say he is 'righteous'. In the mind of the Hebrews, the righteousness (*sedaqah* in

Hebrew) and the well-being went together. Nowadays we can distinguish between them and separate them. We can envisage someone who is rich but certainly does not deserve it, and on the other hand we can accept that goodness may not produce health and wealth, that it may actually have the opposite effect; but the Hebrews could not. They had a 'Covenant God' who had told them they would prosper if they obeyed his commands, but would experience pestilence and other misfortunes if they did not (Leviticus 26:14-16; Deuteronomy 28:21-23, 27-29, 34-35). So righteousness and health, material wellbeing and peace went together, or at any rate they *should* have done so.

This is a description of one of the most salient features of the Old Testament landscape: *shalom.* The word, which occurs more than 250 times in the Hebrew Bible, is usually translated 'peace'. When we speak of peace today we mean little more than an absence of strife and conflict, whereas for the Hebrews it meant all those things in the picture above: prosperity, health, harmony, wisdom and righteousness. *Shalom*, it could be argued, is the Old Testament equivalent of health, and interestingly it comes close to the World Health Organisation's 1948 definition of health: 'Health is a state of complete physical, mental and social wellbeing, and not merely the absence of disease or infirmity.'

But health, of course, breaks down. When a plague came upon the people of Israel, the first question that was asked concerned what the people had been doing wrong that God had brought the sickness upon them. Having found the answer, they had to take steps to right the wrong, and then the sickness would go away. There are seven or so examples of this in the Old Testament. For instance, while the Israelites were wandering in the Wilderness of Sinai under the leadership of Moses, there was rebellion led by a man called Korah; and God responded by sending a plague which killed fourteen thousand seven hundred people. Dr John Wilkinson has suggested that it might have been bubonic plague or cholera.

Moses' brother, the priest Aaron, came and 'stood between the living and the dead', and the plague stopped.

But the people did also make use of doctors. The term for a physician was *rophe,* which derived from the verb 'to mend'. People's bodies could be mended (Genesis 20:17; Exodus 21:19; 2 Chronicles 30:20), as could things (1 Kings 18:30; Jeremiah 19:11). Water could be purified (2 Kings 2:22; Ezekiel 47:8, 9). Even the land itself could be healed (2 Chronicles 7:12-14.), but the physician's function was confined to the body. Physicians are not often mentioned in the Old Testament and one does wonder how much status they had, especially when compared with their influence in Egypt or Mesopotamia. In 2 Chronicles 16:12 we are told how Asa, King of Judah, died because 'he did not seek help from the Lord, but only from the physicians'. However, in fairness to the doctors, we ought to note that the point of the story seems to be not that Asa should have relied entirely upon God, but that he *only* made use of medical help. He used 'pills' (or whatever corresponded to them in those days) without using 'prayers' as well.

Whatever might have been the status of physicians in Old Testament times, there is evidence that their position improved in the centuries between the last writings of the Old Testament and the writing of the New. The most telling piece of evidence comes from a book called Ecclesiasticus (not to be confused with the Old Testament book called Ecclesiastes). Ecclesiasticus was written by one Jesus ben Sirach, who lived in Jerusalem in the second century BCE. Sirach had this to say about physicians:

'Honour a physician according to thy need of him with the honour due unto him;
For verily the Lord hath created him.
For from the most high cometh healing;
And from the King he shall receive a gift.
The skill of the Physician shall lift up his head;
And in the sight of great men he shall be admired.'
(Ecclesiasticus 38:1)

For Sirach, the skill of the physician and the substances he uses are all part of God's creation, put there for the purpose of healing.

Anyone turning to the Old Testament, expecting to find it studded with healing miracles like the New Testament, will be disappointed. There are many miracles of divine deliverance, and numerous instances of God doing the opposite of healing and sending plagues upon people, but very few healing miracles. On the whole, the great prophets (i.e. men and women commissioned to bring the people messages from God) are not depicted doing healings. (Isaiah heals King Hezekiah's 'boil' with a poultice of figs in 2 Kings 20:1-7, but this is probably a folk-remedy.) There are, however, two exceptions to this, namely, Elijah and Elisha (not to be confused with each other), whose exploits are described in the last chapters of the first book of Kings and the first chapters of the second. The two prophets, whose careers overlapped one another, lived in the northernmost of the two kingdoms into which Israel split after the death of King Solomon.

The stories told about the two men have immense drama and power, and include healing miracle stories such as the story of Elisha's healing of Naaman, the King of Syria's General, in 2 Kings 5:1-15.

It is strange that the healing miracles of the Old Testament should be confined to the ministries of these two great prophets, and this requires an explanation. A sceptic might say that these stories are legends of the kind that grow up around great historical personages. Whereas most of the prophets left records in writing, thereby keeping the record straight, Elijah and Elisha left none, and this allowed legends to accumulate around them in a way they never could with, say, an Isaiah or an Ezekiel.

However, there is another explanation for this sudden crop of healing miracles. The ninth century BCE was a time when faith in the one true God hung in the balance. There had always been a tendency for paganism to take over Israel in one way or another. But in the time of King Ahab, in whose reign the ministry of Elijah began, things came to a head. Ahab married a woman called Jezebel, a princess of Sidon. Not content to practise paganism herself, Jezebel was evangelical about it, and wished Israel to turn pagan too. Elijah successfully challenged her, and in so doing was a major factor in preserving Israel's faith. His successor Elisha had better relations with royalty, but the need remained for monarch and people to be reminded that there was no God in all the world except the God of Israel. This meant that they not only had to be told about the power and sovereignty of God, they had to be shown it. Hence the power of God was displayed in miracles. It was a time of 'power encounter'. Elijah's greatness led to a tradition that Elijah would return before the Messiah would come (Malachi 4:5).

This leads us to another important feature of the Old Testament landscape. For the men who wrote the Old Testament, history was incomplete, and there was a better time yet to come. That time is described in various ways. A prophet/priest/ king figure would come, namely, the Messiah, which is Hebrew for the 'Anointed One'. (The word 'Christ' [*Christos*] means the same in Greek.) The best-known predictions of the Messiah are Isaiah 9:2-7 and 11:1-9. Isaiah 9, verse 6, describes him as 'the Prince of Peace', that is, the Prince of *Shalom.* In another passage (Isaiah 53), Isaiah depicts him as a mysterious suffering figure, and tells us, hauntingly, 'by his wounds we have been healed.'

Another feature of the future would be a 'New Covenant'. A covenant means something like an agreement, and the old agreement made between God and Israel on Mount Sinai in the time of Moses had as its basis the idea that if Israel were faithful to God, obeying him in all things, he for his part would take care of them. Unfortunately, Israel found it extraordinarily difficult to keep its part of the agreement, and as a consequence things went wrong in both its personal life and its national life (Isaiah 59:1-4). The great prophet

Jeremiah saw most clearly that one day there would be – would *have* to be – a 'New Covenant', and by this covenant people's hearts would be changed so that they would have the Law of God within them, and live it spontaneously (Jeremiah 31:31-34).

Thirdly, in time to come there would be an outpouring of the Holy Spirit. Many Christians cling fondly to the belief that every human being has, within him or her, the Holy Spirit of God. One could very much wish that this were true, but both Testaments of the Bible teach otherwise. People do not have the Spirit within them purely by virtue of being members of the human race. If they are to have God living within them, God will have to give them his Holy Spirit. In Old Testament times rank and file Israelites did not have the Spirit within them: he was given only to prophets and those called by God to be leaders of the people. In time to come, however, it would be otherwise, and the Spirit would be poured out 'on all flesh'. The prophet Ezekiel hints at this in his unforgettable vision of a great river of water flowing out of the Temple at Jerusalem and bringing life to all the land (Ezekiel 47:1-12).

For the student of healing it is interesting that Ezekiel sees trees growing along the bank of this great river and their leaves are for healing. It appears that healing by natural means will be a by-product of this outpouring. We are also reminded of the 'living water' which Jesus offered in John's Gospel, chapter four, to the outcast woman at the well. The most notable prediction of the Spirit's outpouring, however, comes from Joel, one of the lesser-known prophets, who writes:

'And afterwards,
I will pour out my Spirit on all people.
Your sons and your daughters will prophesy,
Your old men will dream dreams
Your young men will see visions.
Even on my servants, both men and women,
I will pour out my Spirit in those days.'
Joel 2:28, 29.

All these visions of the future, the New Testament tells us, were to become reality in Jesus. He is the Messiah, the One who was to come (John 4:25, 26). He is the strange 'Suffering Servant' of Isaiah 53, fulfilling that prophecy through his death on the Cross (Acts 8:30-35). He inaugurated the New Covenant (Luke 22:20), and the promised 'outpouring' of the Holy Spirit took place soon after Jesus returned to heaven (Acts 2:1-4; 14-21).

Healing is linked with most of these things; and the prophet Malachi, in what is not only the last chapter in his little book but also the very last chapter in the entire Old Testament, says:

'Surely the day is coming; it will burn like a furnace. All the arrogant and every evildoer will be stubble, and that day that is coming will set them on fire,' says the Lord Almighty. 'Not a root or a branch will be left to them. But for you who revere my name, the sun of righteousness will rise with healing in its wings. And you will go out and leap like calves released from the stall.' Malachi 4:1, 2.

Obstacles to entry

Many people today – Christians among them – find that there are intellectual barriers preventing them from exploring healing in the Bible. Therefore, before we go any further, it is important to identify these barriers and see if they can be removed. Even if you are a person of simple faith, it is important to remember that there are many who are not where you are, and you may from time to time find yourself in the position where you need to provide answers for someone else. So it may still be useful to read this section.

Even if there were no miracle stories in the New Testament, there would still be much to learn from it concerning health and healing. We shall discover this as we go along. At the same time, however, we cannot avoid the miracle stories, because they are a huge feature of the Gospels and the Acts of the Apostles. Mark in particular devotes thirty-one per cent of his gospel to them. In the other gospels the proportion is smaller, more space being given to teaching and controversy but, even there, miracles remain so important that we cannot ignore them. And here lies a difficulty experienced by many Christians as well as people of no faith. There seem, in fact, to be several problems, all tied up with one another:

❏ Could miracles happen?
❏ Did Jesus actually perform miracles?
❏ Can we trust the individual miracle stories in the New Testament?
❏ Even if we can answer yes to all the previous three questions, can we still expect miracles of healing today?

Let's take a look at these questions

Could miracles happen?

For modern Western people (although not necessarily for post-modern Western people or inhabitants of the developing world) miracles can seem absurd and impossible, because they break the God-ordained laws of nature.

Physics and astronomy have revealed a universe of breathtaking vastness and complexity, and one which actually turns out not to be predictable where the behaviour of atomic particles is concerned. Perhaps, therefore, assuming that we believe in God, we can accept that God *could* do miracles. If he created this incredible cosmos, is it beyond belief that he might be able to alter it or intervene in it if he chooses to do so? He could, perhaps; but then another question arises: *would* he? Would not a faithful, wise and just God leave the laws of his universe unbroken?

The first reaction of many people would be, 'Of course he wouldn't break his laws.' In this case, the gospel miracles would have to be dismissed as legends or stories that admitted of another explanation. But before you reach this conclusion, reflect on this illustration:

Imagine that you run a drop-in centre in the heart of a big city teeming with social problems. People with all manner of problems and woes drop in to your centre and are welcomed with a cup of tea and are given support and practical help. The centre has certain *rules* which you as the manager were responsible for framing, and one of these rules, which you normally try to stick to, is that the centre opens at 10 am and closes at 4 pm, Monday to Friday. One Friday afternoon you have just seen off the last of the clients and locked up, and you are tidying up before going home, when you hear someone pounding on the door. Peering out through a window you see a young woman on the doorstep. She has with her two small children, one in a ramshackle buggy and one on foot. They are poorly clad, have tearstained faces and runny noses, and the woman herself, scruffily dressed, is in tears and has a black eye and a cut face. Now what do you do? If you are a caring person can you really call through the letterbox that the centre is closed now, that the rules of the centre prohibit you from opening up, and she should come back at ten on Monday morning? Or should you forget about the rules, which, after all, you were responsible for framing, and open up again, saying, 'Come on in. God bless you. You look in a bad way. Let's get you a cup of tea and see what we can do to help.' It's hard to say that love would not break the rules in a case like that. It might be wrong not to break them.

Now, in the place of you, the manager, read God. Nearly all the miracles of the gospels and Acts in which laws of nature are apparently broken occur to people in the direst need, people at the end of their tether. Starving crowds; fishermen in danger of perishing in a storm; leprosy sufferers, whose condition is a living death; demonised persons tormented out of their minds; the widow who has lost her only son: these are the people for whom Jesus works miracles. Jesus might have cured colds and headaches, but there is no record of it. The miracles tend (and the word is used deliberately, because we cannot say God would never do small miracles, and it is many people's experience that he does) to happen when people like the woman in the illustration above call urgently upon God, and God breaks the rules for them.

Hopefully, this has at least put a question mark against the idea that God would not do miracles.

Did Jesus actually perform miracles?

Biblical scholars are not unanimous. When keen Christians come to biblical studies for the first time, it can come as a shock to discover how sceptical many scholars are concerning the authenticity of some of Jesus' sayings and acts. Many of the accounts of the words and deeds of Jesus were transmitted by word of mouth before they were committed to writing, and it is claimed that during that period they were extensively added to or modified. However, there would appear to be many other scholars, apparently equally learned, who feel able to take a more conservative view and offer interpretations of the evidence which support the reliability of the stories and sayings.

So when I first began the research which led to the writing of this book, I expected to find that many biblical scholars would reject all the healing stories of Jesus as legends and fabrications. And it was with considerable surprise that I discovered that scholars, sceptical and conservative, were virtually unanimous that Jesus must have had a remarkable healing ministry. For instance, it is interesting to look at what the great scholar Joachim Jeremias has to say about the authenticity of Jesus' healing ministry. He actually whittles down the miracle stories by suggesting that some of them are 'doublets', or two versions of the same story reported as if they were two different stories. He also claims that some of them arose from misunderstandings, or from people having elaborated stories into miracle stories that were not miracle stories to begin with. And yet, at the end of the day, he is able to list a series of passages which leave him in no doubt that Jesus was a remarkable healer. It would be tedious to list all his evidence, but he mentions in particular the long series of miracles in Mark's gospel, chapters one and two, which clearly have their sources in eye-witness testimony.

Jeremias is only one example out of many. There is a great deal more evidence that I could offer. Suffice it to say that we know beyond reasonable doubt that Jesus of Nazareth did exercise a remarkable healing ministry.

Are the miracle stories reliable?

This is a different question from the previous one.

It could be the case that Jesus had, indeed, a remarkable healing ministry, but that most of the stories about him cannot be relied upon, because so much about him has been altered so that *exactly* what happened, what he did and how he did it, is inaccessible to us. And, of course, if we are to learn much from studying Jesus' healing ministry, we need to have some confidence that what we are reading is reliable. Can we have such confidence?

I believe that Jesus walked on water. However, I take that on trust: I simply believe it. I cannot even begin to prove to the readers of this book that he did so. And this is true of many of the things that Jesus is reported to have said and done. There is no evidence *for* their authenticity, and there is, in some cases, what can be taken as evidence *against*. It is up to the reader to decide whether or not she is prepared to take on trust those stories whose reliability cannot be proven.

Yet it also has to be said that this is *not true* of many of the stories. It isn't anybody's guess whether they are true or not, for there are various tests that can be applied to the stories and sayings to test their authenticity. Let's take a look at some of those tests.

Archaeological evidence

This does have its limitations when it comes to checking the gospel stories. These are not stories about battles and armies, kings and conquests, gods and goddesses, but about ordinary people and their personal encounters with Jesus. Archaeology might confirm, for instance, that Pontius Pilate, the Roman

Governor on whose orders Jesus was executed, was indeed Governor of Judaea in Jesus' time, and it does, actually. But it does not enable us to check out the conversations that Pilate had with Jesus. What it can do, on the other hand, is provide supporting evidence that the background of the story is accurate. In a few stories this evidence is very telling, such as in the case of the healing of the man at the Bethesda Pool.

Linguistic evidence

Jesus did not speak Hebrew. It was already an ancient language when he walked the Earth. Neither did he speak Greek as a first language, though this is the language in which the New Testament was written, but he might well have had some knowledge of it because it was the 'lingua franca' of the entire Eastern Roman Empire, and his native Galilee was a cosmopolitan kind of place. His native tongue was Aramaic, which resembled Hebrew but was quite distinct from it. Now when Aramaic is translated into Greek, or English for that matter, the translation keeps certain characteristics which indicate to us that the story we are reading was originally told in Aramaic, for instance, the use of 'and' (and he went there . . . and he said to them . . . and there was a great storm . . . , etc) or an expression like 'son of'. Aramaic was short of adjectives, so if it wished to say that someone was quick-tempered, for example, it might say, 'He was a *son of* thunder', and so on. These and many other characteristics may indicate that a saying or story was originally uttered in Aramaic. In this way we know that it was told by someone very close to the event it relates, which counts towards its accuracy.

Multiple attestation

This refers to the situation where the same story appears in more than one source; and just as in a law court more than one witness corroborating a story would weigh heavily with a jury, so more than one source would count for a story's authenticity.

Dissimilarity

Perhaps the most technical of the criteria. How it works is this. The scholar asks of a particular story or saying two questions. First of all, could this saying or story have been uttered by a rabbi of Jesus' day? Secondly, could the early Christians have invented it? If the answer to both these questions is 'no', then it is beyond reasonable doubt that the story is authentic.

It is interesting to apply this criterion to the miracle stories. A Jesuit scholar called McGinley examined twenty-one healing stories attributed to rabbis. He found that in no case was an attitude of *faith* required of the patient. This is, of course, in stark contrast to the New Testament healings where recovery is most often bound up with faith. So the stories are *dissimilar* to Jewish stories of the time. But what about the Gentile world, where ideas and stories might have influenced the Christian Church's thinking? Might not the early Christians have picked up some ideas from there and passed them into the tradition? There was a considerable 'healing industry' among the Greeks, centred on pagan shrines, most notable of which was the temple of the god Asclepius at Epidavros, south of Corinth on the Greek mainland. To patronise this shrine was not a particularly pleasant experience. You would sleep there overnight, and serpents would come and crawl over you! There was an attitude required of the patient, and that was *elpis (*hope). It was also said, when recovery was witnessed, that 'seeing is believing'. At first glance, this seems similar to the faith about which Jesus taught, but on closer scrutiny you realise that it isn't. A positive attitude of hope may be helpful (isn't it always?) but that isn't the same as the active faith that Jesus' patients showed when they did things like taking the roof off or grasping the edge of his robe. And again, 'seeing is believing' is a case of, 'first we see the remarkable healing and then we believe', whereas Christian faith says, 'first we believe and then we see the remarkable healing'. So Jesus' teaching and practice of healing is *dissimilar* to any other healing practices and teachings of his time; and that counts for its authenticity. It is exciting to see miracle stories passing these tests.

Verisimilitude

J. B. Phillips, a pioneer in putting the New Testament into modern English, once wrote a book called *The Ring of Truth*, in which he showed how time and again the stories of the gospels have a true-to-life character. Of course, opinions are bound to differ as to whether or not a particular incident is true to life. When Jesus healed a man born blind, John records that *'His neighbours and those who had formerly seen him begging asked, "Isn't this the same man who used to sit and beg?" Some claimed that he was. Others said, "No, he only looks like him" ' (John 9:8, 9)*. Not everyone reading this passage will think that this is a life-like touch, but many will, and if enough people find enough passages true-to-life, this will help to establish the accuracy of the record.

Eye-witness testimony

This is not the same as verisimilitude. It means that some stories have features, other than their being true-to-life, which indicate the presence of an eye-witness. The most obvious example is the famous 'we' passages of the Acts of the Apostles, where the narrator says things like, 'We went to such and such a place and we did this or that.' Here is no second- or third-hand story. The narrator, probably Luke himself, is able to say, like the Welsh entertainer Max Boyce, 'I know 'cos I was there.' In the gospels, too, we shall find many passages where some remark, or some feature of the story, suggests the presence of an eye-witness. This is particularly true of Mark's Gospel, and fits in with an old tradition that Mark derived a lot of his information from Simon Peter.

On the whole, we are on firm ground in believing that not only did Jesus have a remarkable healing ministry, but that we can also learn much about how he conducted it.

Can we expect miracles to happen today?

There is a school of thought in Christianity known as 'cessationism'. It has no problem with the idea of the miraculous, and has no problem either with the reliability of the healing stories, but denies that healings still happen today, on the ground that they are no longer meant to happen. For this school of thought, miracles belonged to the time of the ministry of Jesus and the lifetime of the apostles, but we should not expect them to happen nowadays.

Cessationism has some very weighty theologians behind it. Theologians do not come any weightier than the great sixteenth-century Church reformer John Calvin, who wrote in Book Four of his *Institutes of the Christian Religion*: '*The gift of healing disappeared with the other miraculous powers which the Lord was pleased to give for a time, that it might render the new preaching of the Gospel for ever wonderful. Therefore, even were we to grant that anointing was a sacrament of those powers that were then administered by the hands of the Apostles, it pertains not to us, to whom no such powers have been committed.*'

The other great sixteenth-century reformer Martin Luther wrote in his *Sermons on John 14-16*: '*Now that the Apostles have preached the Word, and have given their writings, and nothing more than what they have written remains to be revealed, no new and special miracle is necessary.*'

Luther was to change his mind on this in later years, but Calvin apparently did not, and his view (which did not originate with him) remained for centuries almost the official line in many churches. Even as late as 1960, a report on glossolalia, or 'speaking in tongues', made to the Bishop of Los Angeles, had this to say:

'*The abnormal physical and psychological phenomena which attracted much attention on the day of Pentecost tended to disappear within the body of Christ, and at the last seemed to have died out. The Whitsunday phenomena could be com-*

pared to the scaffolding surrounding an edifice. Once the edifice (the Church) had been completed, the scaffolding became unnecessary and was discarded. "When I was a child, I spoke as a child, but when I became a man I put away childish things" (1 Cor. 13:11). The glossolalia occurred in the infancy of the Church. With her growth and maturity the Church wisely discarded the marks of infancy.'

True, that report was not specifically about healing, yet speaking in tongues, as we shall see, is closely linked with healing, and is listed by Paul in 1 Corinthians 12 as one of the gifts of the Spirit. Cessationism is still at work here.

Ironically, 1960 was also the year the Charismatic Movement appeared. It began quite specifically in Revd Dennis Bennet's church at Van Nuys, near Los Angeles, and from there spread throughout the worldwide church, promoting and demonstrating the gifts of the Spirit, which, of course, included healing. For people who found physical or emotional health through this movement, yet who wanted to remain loyal to their own churches, cessationism might well have made them feel as if they were waiting, frustrated, at the boundary of the territory of healing, accompanied by a whole convoy of human need, yet needing to produce the right documentation to enable them to go through.

Can this 'documentation', as it were, be provided? There is not space in a book of this kind to explain in detail a huge, centuries-long debate; but here are some important points:

One form of cessationist argument says that apostles were a particular class of people whose role belonged only to the first generation after Jesus. The gift of healing was a mark of the apostle (Romans 15:18; 2 Corinthians 2:12; Mark 16:17, 18; Acts 2: 43; 5:12), but it was not a mark of the Church in general.

This argument is complicated by the fact that there is a lot of uncertainty about what apostles were. We know that the word means 'one who is sent', but whether it refers only to the twelve original disciples, or to other people ordained or called by God to a kind of missionary leadership, is much debated. For people on the Roman Catholic wing of the Church, bishops are the successors of the apostles. Are we to understand, therefore, that all bishops should display healing gifts? In this book we will assume that healing gifts were not confined to apostles, for if they *were* confined to apostles, whoever they were, why do we find Ananias (not an apostle) healing Saul of Tarsus by the laying on of hands in Acts 9, and Philip the Evangelist (Acts 8) and Stephen (Acts 6:8) performing healings and wonders, even though they are nowhere named as apostles. Why, too, does Paul mention 'healers' in the Church (1 Corinthians 12:28) along with all other kinds of gifts of the Spirit, as if healing is likely to be found, like the other gifts, in ordinary people? And again, why does James 5:13-16 suggest calling upon the elders of the Church to come and anoint sick people with oil and pray for them, adding that 'the prayer of faith' will save the sick person, as if the power of healing is located in the prayers of the Church and not in the apostles?

Another point at issue arises from something that is said in one of the most-loved chapters in the New Testament: 1 Corinthians 13, the great chapter on love. Bear in mind that this chapter is usually read on its own, out of context, with the result that the verses in question are not fully understood. The context is that in 1 Corinthians 12 Paul has been talking about the gifts of the Spirit, of which healing is one, and also knowledge, and prophecy and speaking in other tongues, etc., and he has clearly written the chapter because the Corinthian Christians (who were a turbulent, unruly bunch) were exercising these gifts very freely and *priding* themselves on being able to exercise the gifts. There seems to have been a tendency for individuals to regard themselves as superior to others, more 'mature', somehow, because they exercised certain gifts that others did not. This was causing discord, and there was a serious lack of love.

Paul also wants to point out that being proud of oneself

because one has certain gifts is not a sign of maturity as a Christian, but of immaturity. This is why he writes this chapter, and it should be borne in mind as we look at the following verses from it.

'Love never fails. But where there are prophecies, they will cease; where there are tongues, they will be stilled; where there is knowledge, it will pass away. For we know in part and we prophesy in part, but when perfection comes, the imperfect disappears. When I was a child, I talked like a child, I thought like a child, I reasoned like a child. When I became a man, I put childish ways behind me. Now we see but a poor reflection as in a mirror; then we shall see face to face. Now I know in part; then I shall know fully, even as I am fully known' (13:8-12).

When Paul says that prophecies, tongues and knowledge will pass away, when does he envisage this happening? A cessationist might say that this was to happen when the canon was formed. The term 'canon' has nothing to do with a certain rank of Anglican clergy, but means the official list, if you like, of books that make up the New Testament. The Church has always regarded the books which make up that final list as being the ultimate authority for all that we believe as Christians. So on this view Paul is saying, 'We shall not need all this prophesying and tongue-speaking and teaching, because all that we need will be there in the book which God will cause to be put together.' Healing and miracles, of course, are not mentioned, and you could argue that they would not be affected by the formation of the New Testament, because they have nothing to do with knowledge or information. At the same time, however, the gifts of the Holy Spirit are a kind of package (as we shall see later when we come to look at 1 Corinthians 12), and the more we study or experience them, the less likely it seems that some would be torn away and the others left intact.

The other interpretation of the verse is that the time when

knowledge will vanish away is when we get to Heaven. None of these gifts will be needed then, because we shall see God face to face (13:12), and the only thing that will last into Heaven is love.

How are we to choose between these two interpretations? It isn't totally easy, because Paul has not been talking either about the afterlife or the formation of the canon. The latter lay years in the future, and if this was what he meant, you would think he would explain himself. As the verse stands, if he was referring to the canon, his readers would be most puzzled as to his meaning. On the other hand they probably did have some idea that what he meant by 'now . . . and then' was this life and the afterlife, and if they didn't, chapter 15 of 1 Corinthians would soon put them in the picture, being all about the life to come.

Another controversial verse is verse 11, about growing up and putting childish things behind you. Our cessationist friend would say that this means that in the period of Christianity's infancy, Christianity might have needed all these childish things to get going, but when it had grown up and become well-established, wise and mature, it would not have needed them any longer. The conflicting interpretation is that Paul means that it is childish to *pride ourselves* on having spiritual gifts, and if we are truly mature (and loving) we should not be proud of ourselves but use the gifts to the glory of God.

Again, the second interpretation is the more likely, because it fits into the context of the Corinthians behaving childishly. He urges them to become mature as individuals, not as a church. He doesn't say, 'when *we* have grown up, we will put away childish things', but, 'when *I* have grown up'. He is talking about individual behaviour, showing off, immaturity and a lack of love.

So we should not take this chapter as meaning that spiritual gifts will die out before Christ comes again. Paul is saying something quite different about personal gifts, maturity, and the importance of love in the fellowship.

Apart from this chapter, the reader will search the New Testament in vain for other passages which suggest that healing or any other spiritual gift will die out.

Did healing, miracles and the other gifts of the Spirit die out as the Church grew older? There must certainly have been lengthy periods when their existence was not exactly obvious, otherwise cessationism would not have convinced so many people; but they never seem to have died out completely. For example, in 731 the Venerable Bede, a Northumbrian monk of immense learning, wrote his *History of the English Church and People*. Even today it makes for an exciting read, detailing many miraculous events, and reading at times like a piece of charismatic 'testimony literature' set in the Dark Ages. Again, many centuries later, in the journal of the eighteenth-century horseback evangelist John Wesley, no fewer than forty-four healings are described – forty-five if we count a healing of his horse!

These are very far from being the only examples, and yet there do seem to have been long periods of 'silence'. To some extent this is how things seem, not how they were, because church historians, wanting to retain their reputations as objective historians, must really find it difficult to incorporate miracle stories into their work. Few writers on John Wesley mention the healing stories in his *Journal*. Yet the dearth of miracles, prophecies, et cetera, isn't a totally false impression.

Morton Kelsey has sought to explain the disappearance of the more unusual gifts of the Spirit in the history of the Church. There is not the space here to go into all that he has to say, because that is another country and another journey, if you like, but it is probably true that after the Roman Emperor Constantine made Christianity the official religion of the Empire, it quickly became a faith that it was a social advantage to belong to, rather than a faith which might cost Christians their lives or liberty. This must have meant a massive reduction in fervour and commitment and prayerfulness.

In the earlier centuries of the Church's life, however, Kelsey makes it clear that a different state of affairs prevailed, and in his book *Healing and Christianity* he lists statements from many writers of the first four centuries of Christianity which mention healing and miracles, one of the most telling being found in the book *The Shepherd of Hermas*:

'He that knows the calamity of (a sick) man and does not free him from it, commits a great sin, and is guilty of his blood.'

Of course, the stories that such writers tell could well have been legendary. That may be so, but the point is that they did still expect healings and miracles to occur. They had no notion of a time coming when they would stop.

Finally, it is important to remember Jesus' words in John 14:12:

'I tell you the truth, anyone who has faith in me will do what I have been doing. He will do even greater things than these, because I am going to the Father.'

Equipment necessary

Bible software is useful, enabling you to compare different passages on screen. Failing that, you would be greatly helped by a good modern translation of the Bible, preferably the New International Version (NIV), which is the one used and quoted in this guide, or the New Revised Standard Version. Also useful is a caring heart, an open mind, and a desire to know more about the things of God.

section 2
A tour of the healing stories in the Gospels

A preliminary briefing

All the healing miracle stories in the gospels are commented upon in the section that follows. The healing miracles are obviously not the only miracles the gospels relate. There are also so-called 'nature miracles' like the Feeding of the Five Thousand or the Stilling of the Storm. These are often treated as a separate category, when they aren't really, because the miraculous healing of someone's body is every bit as much a nature miracle as any of the others. The reason for leaving the nature miracles out, apart from space, is that this book is specifically about the healing of the body and the personality. However, we do need to bear in mind that, strictly speaking, we should not divide up the miracle stories in that way.

The section also includes a number of stories which are not healing miracles as such, but are best described as healing encounters. So, because these stories are full of meaning and because we wish to make clear a)that mind as well as body can be healed and b) that a lot of healing does not involve breaking nature's laws, we have included them.

The same healing stories do not occur in all four gospels, but quite a good number occur in three, a few in only two, and quite a large number in only one. The way the following 'itinerary' works is as follows:

Firstly, all the healing miracles described in Mark are taken in order, and the parallel stories in the other two gospels are examined at the same time. Next, the healings recorded in Matthew's gospel but not in Mark's are described in the order in which they occur in his book, and where there is a parallel story, not in Mark, but in Luke, that is dealt with at the same time. Then come the stories which occur only in Luke's gospel, and finally those which occur only in John's. Then we go back to the beginning and tackle a few 'healing encounters'.

Healing miracle stories

	Matthew	Mark	Luke	John
1 Synagogue Demoniac	-	1:21-28	4:31-37	-
2 Peter's Mother-in-law	8:14, 15	1:30, 31	4:38, 39	-
3 Leprosy cured	8:2-4	1:40-42	5:12, 13	-
4 Paralysed Man	9:2-8	2:3-12	5:17-26	-
5 Man with withered hand	12:9-14	3:1-6	6:6-11	-
6 Gadarene Demoniac	8:28-34	5:1-17	8:26-39	-
7 Woman with a Haemorrhage	9:20-22	5:24-34	8:43-48	-
8 Jairus's Daughter	9:18, 19, 23, 26	5:22-24, 35-43	8:40-42, 49-56	-
9 Syro-Phoenician Girl	15:21-28	7:24-30	-	-
10 Deaf & Dumb Man	-	7:31-37	-	-
11 Blind Man of Bethsaida	-	8:22-26	-	-
12 Boy with 'epilepsy'	17:14-18	9:14-27	9:38-43	-
13 Blind Bartimaeus	20:29-34	10:46-52	18:35-43	-
14 Centurion's Servant	8:5-13	-	7:1-10	-
15 Two Blind Men	9:27-31	-	-	-
16 Dumb Demoniac	9:32-34	11:1-14	-	-
17 Blind & Dumb Demoniac	12:22	-	-	-
18 Widow's Son	-	-	7:11-17	-
19 Mary Magdalene	-	-	8:2	-
20 Bent Woman	-	-	13:10-13	-
21 Man with Dropsy	-	-	14:1-4	-
22 Ten Leprosy cases	-	-	17:11-19	-
23 Malchus' Ear	-	-	22:49-51	-
24 Nobleman's Son	-	-	-	4:46-53
25 Lame Man at Pool	-	-	-	5:1-9
26 Man Born Blind	-	-	-	9:1-7
27 Lazarus	-	-	-	11:1-44

Healing encounters

28 Zacchaeus	-	-	19:1-10	-
29 The Woman at the Well	-	-	-	4:4-30
30 The Restoration of Simon Peter	-	-	-	21:1-19

1 The Synagogue Demoniac
(Mark 1:21-28; Luke 4:31-37)

Jesus began his ministry as he meant to go on. In the opening phase of his ministry he appears to have based himself in the little town of Capernaum on the north-west shore of the Sea of Galilee. In most of the towns and villages of Galilee there would have been synagogues, 'places of gathering together', where Jews would gather on a Saturday (the Sabbath) to pray and to listen to sermons in which the Law, the Prophets and the Writings of the Old Testament would be explained and applied to life. Any adult male might be allowed to speak, but what he said had to be on the authority of others: what Rabbi so-and-so said about the passage, and what Rabbi so-and-so said. But when Jesus got up to speak he was different. He appeared to speak on his own authority, which must have thrilled some of his hearers and worried others very much.

But as if to underline his authority, a healing miracle took place in the synagogue right under the noses of the people. There was present a man with an evil spirit in him. Our translation says he was 'possessed' by the spirit, but there is no word for 'possessed' in the original Greek of the passage, nor, for that matter, is the word for 'possessed' ever found in the original Greek of the New Testament in connection with demonisation. It is worth noting that if it had been known that the man had this problem, it is unlikely that he would have been allowed into the synagogue. The demonisation was hidden, and exorcists who operate today will tell you that this is often the case.

If, in addition, this man had had any symptoms of illness, we are not told about them. However, the demon seemed to have been profoundly disturbed by the presence of Jesus, and called out in anguish, revealing that it knew what others did not know, that Jesus is 'the Holy One of God'.

Jesus commanded the demon to be quiet and come out of

the man. In Mark's version of the story we are told that the demon then shook him violently and came out of him with a shriek. Luke, however, leaves out the bit about the shriek and tells us instead that the demon came out of the man 'without harming him'. Jesus didn't torment the man; he healed him, for someone demonised is in need of healing.

What exactly twenty-first century people, especially twenty-first century Westerners, are to make of demonisation and exorcism is tackled in Boxed Byways, under Demons and Deliverance. For the moment, suffice it to say that a remarkable healing *had* taken place, and the congregation were amazed. Mark says they were amazed at Jesus' *authority*. Luke says they were amazed at both his authority *(exousia)* and at his power *(dunamis)*. The word for power is the word from which, of course, we derive the words 'dynamo', 'dynamite' and 'dynamic', which convey the flavour of its meaning.

The story puts healing in its right place; for healing, important though it was, and spectacular though it might have been, was not the most important activity in which Jesus engaged. The most important thing he did was to preach the Gospel and to teach. Healing accompanied that and confirmed it, but not the other way round.

Another thing this story shows us is the power and authority of Jesus over evil. This power, although boundless, nevertheless works through and with his followers. There would, in fact, come a point when the disciples would say, 'Even the devils are subject to us in your name' (Luke 10:17). This is something that ought also to give his present-day followers boundless confidence.

2 The Healing of Peter's Mother-in-Law
(Matt. 8:14, 15; Mark 1:30, 31; Luke 4:38, 39)

This passage, which is surely an eye-witness account, reminds us that Jesus' disciples were not necessarily bachelors. They had families; some would have wives, and perhaps also children, who would have had their own particular sacrifices to make in following Jesus; and in this little story we see Jesus, in a way, keeping faith with a member of a disciple's family. Simon Peter was married, and in later years he apparently took his wife around with him on missionary tours (see 1 Corinthians 9:5). According to Mark, it was 'immediately' on leaving the synagogue that Jesus went to Simon's house. Mark's Jesus does not hang about. There is much to be done and little time to do it. That evening the 'whole town' would be gathered at Simon's door, clamouring for help and healing, and Jesus would be up before dawn next morning praying in a remote place. Hard-pressed aid workers today, or Christian leaders in inner-city situations coping with mountains of human need, can be sure that Jesus knows how they feel, having been there himself. Christ 'leads us through no darker rooms than he went through before'.

At Simon's house, his mother-in-law lay sick with a fever, and Jesus instantly healed her. Mark says he took her hand and helped her up. Matthew says he touched her hand; but Luke, surprisingly, shows Jesus adopting a much more severe stance. He stands over her (or perhaps bends over her) and rebukes the fever. We are accustomed to associate healing with the laying on of hands, but in fact Jesus displays different approaches to different sufferers, and here he surprises us by rebuking the fever. This fits in with Luke's emphasis that sickness is an evil thing, something whose nature is such that it should be rebuked.

A minister I knew in Yorkshire visited a woman apparently terminally ill with cancer. Years later he encountered the same woman at a meeting, and she reminded him of his visit. He could not recall what he had said on that occasion, so she jogged his memory. 'You said, "Cancer be gone", and I improved from then on.'

The immediate sequel to the story before us was that Simon's mother-in-law got up and began to fuss around and get them some lunch! Here is a subtle reminder that we are not healed in order to carry on living a self-indulgent life, following our own plans for our lives instead of God's calling. We are saved to set us free to love and serve others.

3 The Healing of a Man with Leprosy
(Matt. 8:2-4; Mark 1:40-42; Luke 5:12, 13)

This little story seems straightforward enough, but it sets commentators some thorny problems.

Firstly, what exactly was the man suffering from? We usually assume that leprosy in the Bible is the hideous disease often encountered in the developing world today, and characterised by ugly sores, anaesthesia and deformity. However, back in the Old Testament, Leviticus 13 offers comprehensive instructions on how a priest should diagnose a skin disease, which is usually called leprosy, but the identity of which is uncertain. Whatever the identity of the disease, it rendered the sufferer 'unclean', and unless he recovered and was pronounced 'clean' by the priest, he had to live alone, away from human habitations, and avoid contact with other people. He could not die of the disease, but it was a living death.

The other problem concerns Jesus' attitude to the man with leprosy. Here we need to understand that many ancient manuscripts of the New Testament, or parts of it, still exist. Since they were copied out by hand for centuries before the invention of printing, many discrepancies occur in them, and some manuscripts are known to be more reliable than others. One of the rules for establishing the correct reading would be that the more difficult or unlikely a particular reading is, the more likely it is to be correct, because no copyist would alter something to make it weird, but he might well alter something that struck him as weird to make it more sensible. Now, where in Mark 1:41 we find the words 'filled with compassion', some manuscripts say 'filled with anger', and that, being the more difficult reading, is the one the scholar would normally pick. One can imagine a copyist thinking, 'Surely Jesus could not have been filled with anger. It must surely have said "filled with compassion" so I'll alter it to that.'

Then in verse 43, NIV, it says Jesus sent the healed man away with a 'strong warning', and the Greek is even stronger. It says he 'snorted'. With anger, presumably.

Why? There are, it appears, two possibilities. One is that Jesus was annoyed with the leprosy sufferer because the man was not behaving well according to his lights. Luke says he came to Jesus when he was in one of the towns. According to the law, the man should not have been so close to human habitation, so he was being reckless about whom he made unclean, and reckless, too, about making Jesus unclean. Technically, of course, Jesus was made unclean by the encounter, because he touched the man; and it is possible that one reason why Jesus told him not to say anything to anyone was that if he *had* told people, they would have shunned Jesus, too, until he managed to get to Jerusalem and show himself to the priests. If this theory is correct, it took remarkable grace on Jesus' part to touch the man, nevertheless, and to heal him.

Grace in Christian parlance means 'undeserved love', and it always characterises God's dealing with us, because we don't deserve his healing or any of his blessings. The man with leprosy sensed that he was not *entitled* to expect healing, in that he said, 'Lord, *if you will* you can make me clean.' Grace is also something that Christians are required to show to others, and in a way this story reveals what that might mean. Needy people not only pose the problem of looking or smelling bad; their own attitudes may leave much to be desired. They may deliberately, for instance, make dangerous nuisances of themselves, as this man did.

An alternative explanation, less likely but possible, is that Jesus saw sickness as evil, and was angry about what this loathsome disease had done to the man.

One last thing calls for mention before we move on. It may mean that when healing ministry has apparently worked for us, we should have our recovery checked by an expert. In those times it was the priest. Today it is the doctor. Having your healing checked out might seem to indicate a lack of faith, and for that reason some ill-informed people, thrilled by their healing, discontinue their medication or treatment without first checking with a doctor. This passage suggests to me that healing will need to be confirmed.

4 The Paralysed Man
(Matt. 9:1-8; Mark 2:1-12; Luke 5:17-26)

The differences between the three accounts of this charming story of the man let down through the roof are instructive. Matthew follows his usual policy of ruthless abridgement and leaves out altogether the part about the lowering through the roof. Mark says the four friends dug through the plaster of the roof, having gone up by the stairs which gave access to the roofs of Palestinian houses in those days. Luke the Gentile says that they let him down through the tiles, as if it were a Roman style of house. Luke was surely well aware that Galilaean homes were not built that way, but putting it like that perhaps saved him from having to give an unnecessary explanation to Theophilus. Jesus seems unconcerned about the damage, but that could be because he was Capernaum-based at the time, and it could actually have been his own house.

The crowd now includes scribes, that is to say, teachers of the Law, who have come from as far away as Jerusalem: a sign that clouds are gathering. The Jewish authorities are beginning to hear disquieting reports of this charismatic teacher, and have come to check him out. It turns out that they don't like what they hear, unfortunately, and are blind to the wonder of what Jesus does. Sadly, 'religion' can go wrong, and have the effect of stifling the Holy Spirit's work. This is a tendency which is not confined to Judaism. It can happen in Christianity.

Jesus' first gentle words to the paralysed man are, 'Son, your sins are forgiven.' Luke has, 'Friend, your sins are forgiven,' and Matthew makes the statement even more tender with the words, 'Take heart, son, your sins are forgiven.' This must not be taken to imply that Jesus taught that all sickness is the result of the sufferer's sin, but in this case it apparently was. It has been suggested that the man's sickness was hysterical paralysis resulting from his guilt over something that he had done. Alternatively, he may have been a stroke victim, the stroke arising from the stress induced by a sense of guilt. We cannot know for certain.

But the scribes had Jesus down as a blasphemer. They believed that only God could forgive sins, and the possibility that the one standing in front of them might be the Son of God was too much to accept. So to demonstrate that something was happening to make their ideas obsolete, and to confirm his forgiveness of the man, Jesus told him to pick up his stretcher and walk, and he did just that! The forgiveness of God is a far greater miracle than the healing of paralysis, it is true, but the onlookers could not tell simply by looking, whether the man was forgiven or not. It was therefore easier (not *very* easy in that particular company, but *easier*) to *say*, 'Your sins are forgiven', than it was to say, 'Take up your bed and walk.' If the man had not taken up his bed and walked Jesus would have been totally discredited; and the fact that he was so obviously healed confirmed the forgiveness too.

People were amazed and praised God, and one hopes that this included the scribes, but it probably did not. Matthew adds an intriguing tail-piece. He says they praised God, 'who had given such power to *men*.' Matthew is writing about the relationship which believers have with the risen Jesus now, but in the form of a gospel about his earthly life. He implies that the power to do healings will be committed, not just to the Messiah, but to his people too!

5 The Man with the Withered Hand
(Matt. 12:9-14; Mark 3:1-6; Luke 6:6-11)

Jesus had yet another synagogue encounter, this time against a background of increasing hostility. Much of this hostility came from the Pharisees, who were a party within the Jewish nation. Intensely religious, and with a deep desire to serve God (for which we can respect them), they were nevertheless guilty of 'legalism', which can be defined as the belief that God is best served by keeping many regulations, covering every area of life. Jesus strongly opposed legalism (see Matt. 23:23, 24), for Christian morality, rightly understood, differs from legalism in that it takes certain inviolable principles (like justice, compassion, stewardship, and, above all, love) and applies them to different cases in different ways. Legalism tends to be morally 'blind', in that it can completely overlook the need for compassion and genuinely caring behaviour in favour of keeping the rules. Jesus challenges them over this in the question he puts to them in verses 11 and 12 of Matthew's version of this story. If they could haul a sheep out of a pit on the Sabbath (and they could, for the law allowed it) why could they not offer help to the needy in other ways?

In the synagogue there is a man with a withered or 'shrivelled' hand. The Gospel of the Nazaraeans (a book which did not find its way into the New Testament) appears to know a little more about this man, and tells us that he was a 'cementarius', or stonemason. Dr John Wilkinson says that if this is correct then the shrivelled hand, his right hand according to Luke, would have been the result of nerve-damage stemming from the repetitive movement of hammer and chisel. But whatever the problem might have been, the man could not support a wife or any children he might have had. Jesus, always on the move, may never be there again, and his chance of healing would be gone. Should the man be denied healing because of the need to keep the Torah with rigid literalness?

Angry at their attitude, Jesus has the man stretch out his hand, and it is healed. Note once again Jesus' flexibility of approach. He does not even touch the man, let alone 'lay hands on' him. And once again, faith is not mentioned, though that does not rule out the possibility that Jesus might have perceived that the man had faith. Alternatively, Jesus might have been using this miracle as a test case to make a point. If that is the case, the point is not taken, and the Pharisees go off and begin to plot against Jesus. In fact, Mark tells us that they went off and plotted with the Herodians, associates of the decadent King Herod, whom normally the Pharisees would have shunned: an unbelievable thing to do when one considers that what provoked it was the healing of an innocent, needy man. Tom Wright, the scholarly Bishop of Durham, claims that they would have been particularly incensed at this particular violation of the Law because the Sabbath was a major symbol of Jewish identity, almost in the way a flag might be. Jesus was not burning that flag; rather, if you like, redesigning it; however, that was not how they saw it.

I cannot emphasise too strongly that the story is not anti-semitic. It is anti-legalistic. Legalism is a vice which affects Christians too, and is often the enemy of true caring and true healing.

Differences between the Gospels

To get the most from our tour of the Gospels, certain facts about them need to be borne in mind.

Matthew, Mark and Luke differ from John in having a lot of material in common. For this reason they are known as the Synoptic Gospels. ('Synoptic' means 'seen together'). It is an interesting experiment to borrow three copies of the same translation of the Bible (say the New International Version), or some Bible software which enables you to compare Bible passages side by side, and look up Matthew 9:2-8, Mark 2:3-12 and Luke 5:17-26. It will immediately be apparent that the three gospels are not merely telling the same story, but telling it in some places

in exactly the same words! You could carry out the same exercise on many other passages in the first three gospels with exactly the same results, and most biblical scholars are in agreement that this is because Mark wrote his gospel first, and Matthew and Luke then incorporated most of his work into their own books. Matthew and Luke also appear to have another source in common which has not survived on its own, and this is known to scholars as 'Q'. Then the rest of their gospels is made up of material peculiar to themselves. In the case of Matthew, this material is called 'M', and in the case of Luke, 'L'.

John goes his own way, using his own sources and informants. His gospel is judged to have been written some time after the others, and he seems to have wanted to avoid going over the ground that they had already covered.

The gospels differ in *the way they set their material out.* John tells long stories and has long talks and discussions. Some of these are chapter-long, which makes it easy for the Bible student to remember where things are in his gospel (Chapter 3, Nicodemus; chapter 4, the Woman at the Well, etc.). The other gospels tell shorter stories and have shorter sayings, because many of them might have been passed down by word of mouth for some time before they were written down. In *Mark*, however, the stories are told with detail and vigour. He is a storyteller. *Matthew* is well-organised. He shortens all of Mark's stories, concentrating on what he sees as the most important points, and organises his material into large blocks. Chapters 5-7 are teaching; 8-9 healings and miracles; 10, more teaching, and so on. By contrast *Luke*, the longest gospel, is a great swirling kaleidoscope of a book in which miracle follows saying, follows encounter, follows miracle all the way through.

Each gospel writer tells the story from his own angle. *Mark* shows Jesus doing miracles because the people are there, they are in real need and he has the power to help them; and the sheer amount of space he gives to the miracles shows how important they are to him. At the same time, however, he shows how Jesus often seemed to want to keep his movements and deeds a secret, as if all too aware of the possibility that people would misunderstand his mission. There is also a point in the gospel when the miracles cease, and Jesus becomes the 'Suffering Servant' (see the section above on the Old Testament): misunderstood, practically alone, his identity hidden, and ultimately humiliated and tortured to death. And it is *this* Jesus of whom the centurion at the foot of the Cross says, 'Surely, this man was the Son of God!' (Mark 15:39).

Matthew is different again. Jesus in Matthew is a solemn, dignified figure. He is often addressed as 'Lord' (*kyrie*), and people seeking his help often fall down on their knees before him. It is as if Matthew is trying to teach his readers about the relationship they may have *now* with their Lord Jesus, who is God become a man, but telling it to them through the medium of the story about his life. Matthew's is a very Jewish gospel, in his language, the way he handles his material and in the way he takes trouble to show how Jesus fulfils the Old Testament prophecies. But at the same time there is a heart-brokenness about the way his fellow-Israelites have turned

Jesus down and therefore brought automatically upon themselves the destruction of Jerusalem.

Luke, by contrast, is a historian, and his gospel is actually the first volume of a two-part history of the Church, written for his mysterious friend Theophilus (1:1-4), the second volume being the Acts of the Apostles. A physician by profession, he tells the healing stories as if, unlike Matthew, he is interested in the details, which means that his gospel has great value for the student of healing.

Accurate historian though he is, Luke nevertheless has his own angle upon Jesus. His Jesus often comes across as a wild, controversial, prophetic character. Yet he also brings out Jesus' concern for women, for 'little people', for outsiders and people who don't fit in. In addition, he gives the impression that he regards sickness as an evil thing. There is a devil, and all sickness has its real origin with him. Hence, because Jesus has come to deliver us from evil, he spends so much time delivering people from sickness.

John tells us only a handful of healing stories, albeit in some detail. Yet he does not for one moment want to suggest that these were the only miracles that Jesus did, because he says himself that there were many others (John 20:30). John is a true evangelist and tells his readers, 'These are written that you may believe that Jesus is the Christ, the Son of God, and that believing you may find life in his name.' With this end in view, he treats the miracle stories as 'signs'. They are miracles that *point* to truths about God.

Other less striking characteristics of the particular gospels will be pointed out as we go along.

> Do not assume from what has been said above that the gospels contradict one another, or present incompatible pictures of Jesus. A policeman will give one account of a traffic accident, the motorist involved another, the paramedics attending the injured another; the insurance assessor will tell a different story and so will a teenage witness relating the incident to his friends afterwards. All of them will, we hope, be telling the truth, but they will be telling it from their angle and in their way, and with their particular concerns in mind. Only by listening to all their stories would we get a full picture of what went on, and of all the implications that the accident might have. So it is with the four Gospels.

6 The Gadarene Demoniac
(Matt. 8:28-34; Mark 5:1-20; Luke 8:26-39)

Jesus and his disciples have sailed across to the other side of the Sea of Galilee to a country which Matthew calls the country of the Gadarenes: and Mark and Luke, the country of the Gerasenes. What country these names refer to is the subject of a lot of conjecture; and all we really need to know is that this was Gentile territory, for if it had been Jewish territory the inhabitants would not have kept pigs! We do not know why Jesus came here, but it might have been an attempt to get away from the harassment of the crowds in Jewish Galilee.

If it was, it proved abortive, and led instead to one of the most awesome and weird encounters of Jesus' entire ministry: with a demon-possessed man who haunted the local cemetery. (On the question of demonisation and mental illness see the article that follows.) Mark tells the story at length and with drama and vigour, and Luke follows him closely. However, Matthew narrows the story down to only seven verses, and for some unknown reason says that there were actually two demoniacs, making the point that they were so violent that no one could pass that way. R. H. Lightfoot, commenting on this passage, says that the implication is that until the demons were dealt with the Gospel could not pass that way either. If he is right the passage gives support to the view held by some Christians that *places* can be demonised, and the practice of 'cleansing' geographical areas before mission can proceed. It has to be said, however, that apart from this passage there is not much biblical support for this idea.

The demoniac 'adjures Jesus by the most high God'. He is trying thereby to gain mastery over Jesus by using his name, and the term 'most high God' is believed to be a pagan term for the God of Israel: a convincing bit of verisimilitude which might just help some to believe this very strange story. The demons inhabiting the man also plead with Jesus not to torture them before the 'appointed time', by which they mean Judgement Day.

The episode of the pigs, invaded by the demons, running to drown themselves in the lake, may seem to us absurd and unnecessary, but it would convince the demoniac that he was indeed set free. One can well imagine that when dark thoughts occurred again, he would remember that whatever he felt, he had *seen* the demons go. That would have meant reassurance and closure for him. It would also have convinced the onlookers of the power of Jesus over the things that had held their community in bondage.

However, their unexpected reaction was *fear,* which suggests that that Gentile community was collectively in bondage to the occult. Persons affected by the occult today often react with anger or fear to any real sign that God is at work, and I suspect that that was the case there. The man himself begged to be allowed to go with Jesus, but was told to go home and tell his family what God had done for him. He went further: he told everybody. There was no instruction to be silent such as Jesus often gave elsewhere, and that was perhaps because in Jewish territory, publicity meant: a) that Jesus would be too harassed by people wanting healing to be able to preach his message properly; and b) that people would identify him as the Messiah, but then put their own interpretation on this and seek to make him a King or a rebel leader. In Gentile territory there were no such risks, so the healed man is able to give full reign to his desire to share the good news.

This story challenges us both in the area of belief and the area of understanding. It challenges *belief* in that it seems to have been particularly difficult to credit. Many attempts have been made to explain the story away, such as the suggestion that the commotion made by the demoniac panicked the pigs and led to their stampede into the lake, and the story developed from there. Faced with this miracle, I follow the line of 'believing where I cannot prove'.

The story challenges our understanding too. Taken as a whole, what is it saying to us? The clue lies in the context, for in both Mark and Luke the story is the second in a series of four powerful miracle stories. The first of these is a 'nature miracle', the stilling of the storm (Mark 4:35-41; Luke 8:22-25), and the two that follow in both gospels are the healing of the woman with a haemorrhage, and the raising to life of Jairus's daughter. The storm had nearly literally 'scuppered' Jesus' mission, for it placed Jesus' and the disciples' lives in danger; but Jesus rebuked the wind and the sea and there was a calm. The four stories look like a kind of unit to show that Jesus is Lord over nature, over evil, over sickness and over death itself. A wonderful comment on them is Psalm 62:11:

> *'One thing God has spoken,*
> *two things have I heard,*
> *that you, O God, are strong,*
> *and that you, O Lord, are loving.'*

Demons and Deliverance

It may be unhelpful to use the term 'demon possession', because it does not occur in the New Testament, which always talks about 'demonisation' or 'having a demon'. But by whatever name we call it, it presents us with something of a problem. The idea of demons does not pose so much of a challenge for Africans or Asiatics as it does for Western men and women, who leave 'demons' out of their world-picture altogether (or did, until the rise of 'post-modernism'), and consequently do not know what to make of Jesus' exorcisms. The usual explanation offered by commentators is that Jesus in his exorcisms was healing mental illness by another name; and there are two things in favour of that explanation: i) Although there are a number of exorcism stories in the new Testament, there are no stories of Jesus' healing madness as such, and ii) in two of the cases of demonisation in the gospels – the 'epileptic' boy and the Gerasene demoniac – the sufferer does seem to display symptoms of mental or nervous disorder. In the one case it is epilepsy, and in the other, according to Dr Wilkinson, 'acute mania'.

However, the 'mental illness' theory is only a satisfactory explanation if you ignore some important data. If there were a hundred exorcisms described in the New Testament, and no healings of mental illness, you could rightly conclude that it was, indeed, madness under another name, but there are only six or seven such stories, and the gospel writers probably picked them out to tell specially, because they so clearly showed Jesus' mastery over evil. Again, while it is true that some of the stories mention symptoms, others do not, and in the case of the Philippian slave girl (q.v.) there do not appear to have been any symptoms other than the habit of telling fortunes and uttering oracles.

The most important piece of datum is Jesus' words in Matthew 12:28 and Luke 11:20: 'If I drive out demons by the Spirit of God, then the kingdom of God has come upon you.' The only significant difference between Matthew's version of the saying and Luke's is that Luke reports Jesus' words as 'if I by the *finger* of God cast out demons'. Luke's version is what Jesus actually *said,* and Matthew has rewritten it slightly to bring out what Jesus actually *meant*. Matthew's is a very Jewish gospel, and in Judaism you were allowed sometimes to alter the text of scripture like that. The practice was called 'implicit *midrash*'. Apart from this change, biblical scholars are for once virtually unanimous in putting these words down as an authentic saying of Jesus, so we cannot get away from the problem they pose by saying that he never uttered them, for utter them he did!

They do pose a problem for Westerners. Jesus is not putting imaginary quotation marks around the words 'drive out demons', as much as to say, 'If I "drive out demons", as you put it', because if we put the words into their context, we find that they form part of a long argument in which he defends himself against the charge that he cast out demons by 'Beelzebul the prince of demons'. 'How can Satan cast out Satan?' says Jesus. As you read the argument, it becomes clear that he really did believe that he was driving out demons. We could, of course, argue that Jesus was a man of his time and therefore believed in demons like everybody else; but in so many obvious ways he was ahead of his time, so why should he not have been in this respect? In any case, belief in demons and demonisation was not universal in the ancient world. Medical works have survived from that period, by such writers as Celsus and Dioscorides. They all deal with madness and suggest certain cures for it, but do not put it down to demon possession. Luke will have been trained in that tradition, so it is remarkable that he did not re-interpret Jesus' exorcisms as cures of mental illness if that was what they were.

So Jesus did not have to attribute mental illness to demons, and had he done so it would surely make us wonder how he could have been the Son of God, the most significant character in human history, who had come to provide the answer to evil, and yet get the origin of mental illness so wrong. It would also make us wonder how his exorcisms could have been effective. If I were to try telling a schizophrenic or a depressive that his trouble was caused by demons and command the demons to exit, I would not get very far, to say the least! And yet Jesus' exorcisms must have been effective, for, had they not been, his enemies would have lost no time in pointing it out. They could not do that, however, and that was why they had to fall back on the explanation that Jesus cast out demons by the prince of demons.

It appears that four conclusions are inescapable: Jesus carried out what were understood to be exorcisms. He himself understood them to be exorcisms. He believed that they illustrated more clearly than anything else God's power and sovereignty over evil. His exorcisms were effective.

To understand what was going on, I believe that we need to look further afield than Western psychiatry.

Many Christian missionaries working among tribes with 'shamanistic' or 'spirit-inviting' practices have returned home with stories of demonisation. Glanville Martin, a Methodist former missionary known to the author, encountered it in Jamaica, for example, and Robert Peterson, a former missionary with the Overseas Missionary Fellowship, encountered it in Kalimantan on a large scale, only to find that when he described it to audiences back home he met with something close to ridicule. These are personal stories, of course, but there is more solid anthropological evidence as well. Between the wars, a German philosophy professor called T. K. Oesterreich brought out a book called *Possession, Demoniacal and Other*. In this massive tome he surveyed reports on cultures all over the world, as far apart as the South Seas and Northern Russia, and found that where there were Shamanism and 'spirit-inviting' activities, they gave rise to an altered mental state of which he thought that 'demon possession' was an apt description. Oesterreich himself pointed out the similarities between his observations and the state of demonisation described in the gospels. His book is now dated, being offensively anti-semitic in places, but the facts he unearthed still throw a flood of light on the condition Jesus was dealing with. His work has been corroborated by other writers, and leaves one in little doubt that the demonisation that we see in the gospels is not what we would understand as mental illness by another name, but a particular kind of altered mental state. Jesus clearly believed that the origins of that mental state were spiritual.

The fact that ours was not a pagan Shamanistic culture (at least not until recently, witchcraft being actually illegal until 1951), meant that we had little or no experience of the phenomenon, and therefore did not know what to make of Jesus' exorcisms. That state of affairs is sadly changing now, for Western society appears to be passing out of 'modernity' into a more superstitious age. Spiritualism and mediumship have long been known, of course, but there has also been a burgeoning of witchcraft, which has probably made demonisation more common in our own society.

The Bible has surprisingly little to say about demonisation's origins or its nature. The exceptionally superstitious Macedonians in Bible times gave many different names and roles to demons, while the Greeks assumed that they were spirits of the dead. The Bible in its wisdom tells us nothing of this, because fascination with the demonic is deeply unhealthy, and an extensive knowledge of it is unnecessary. The Council Environmental Health Inspector, confronted with a house fetid with rubbish and crawling with rats and maggots, doesn't become fascinated with it, cataloguing it and investigating its origins: he just sees that it is cleaned out immediately. So it should be with a Christian involved in the deliverance ministry.

Perhaps demonisation and mental illness should not be entirely separated. Body, mind and spirit are such an interlinked unity that one can well imagine demonisation causing secondary mental disturbance or physical symptoms. Pastors ought to note that

> different Christian denominations have different rules regarding deliverance ministry, and should acquaint themselves with them.

7 The Woman with the Haemorrhage
(Matt. 9:20-22; Mark 5:25-34; Luke 8:43-48)

Mark loved to tell stories within stories, and this is an example, the main story being the raising of Jairus's daughter, whom Jesus is on his way to heal. This is not as hard a story to swallow as the last miracle we examined. The circumstances are convincing, and the way Jesus says, 'Who touched me?' when the woman grabs his robe, and the disciples reply (in Mark), 'You see the people crowding against you and yet you can ask "who touched me?" ' is vividly true to life.

Jesus tells the woman her faith has 'saved' her. The NIV translation conceals that wording by translating Jesus' words as, 'Your faith has *healed* you', but the word is 'saved', which raises the question, did the evangelists just happen to use the word 'saved' for 'healed' because that was how the word was often used, or did they use it because 'salvation' and 'healing' are pretty much the same thing? Remember that salvation in the New Testament often means 'being saved from sin'.

For the student of healing, this story raises two issues. One is how far we can be healed using objects like the hem of Jesus' garment or Paul's handkerchiefs and aprons (Acts 19:11,12). The Boxed Byway on Objects, Shrines and Sacrament goes into this more deeply, but I should point out here that Jesus does say, 'Your *faith* has saved you.' The woman's healing might have involved a physical act of taking hold of Jesus' garment, but that was not what laid hold of healing; what laid hold of healing was her faith.

The other issue stems from Jesus' being aware 'that power had gone out from him' (Luke 8:46). Does this mean that the person with a healing gift actually transmits divine healing power, almost as if it were electricity? There are certainly those engaged in the ministry of healing whose experience suggests that it does. Cameron Peddie, a Scottish minister who had a remarkable ministry of healing in the 1950s, says in his book *The Forgotten Talent*: 'The person ministering is always conscious of the power passing through him (provided he has developed sufficient pastoral sensitivity) and the patient is aware of its presence from the strange heat or coldness that develops.'

Finally, an amusing feature of the story is that while Mark notes how the woman had spent a lot of money on many doctors and had suffered a lot at their hands but only got worse, Luke, a doctor by trade, leaves that information out!

8 Jairus's Daughter
(Matt. 9:18, 19, 23-26; Mark 5:22-24, 35-43; Luke 8:40-42, 49-56)

I tease my flute-playing daughter by quoting Matthew 9:23, 24 at her: 'When Jesus . . . saw the flute players . . . he said "Go away" '. This is the only detail that Matthew, who as usual tells a much shorter story than Mark and Luke, adds to the story. Jesus put the flute-players out, not just because their presence would not be helpful, but because mourning was inappropriate; death was being overcome.

Jairus had come and pleaded with Jesus to come to his house and heal his daughter. According to Mark, he also asked Jesus to come and lay hands on her, and had little doubt that she would be healed and live. Note carefully that while Jairus asked Jesus to 'lay hands on her', a gesture that usually involves two hands laid flat on the head or the affected part of the body, what Jesus eventually did was simply to take the little girl by the hand. We often prescribe to God what we think he should do, and then he does something quite different. Often, too, ministers, elders or people with a healing ministry will find that either the sufferer or the sufferer's friends and relations will prescribe what they think should be done; but in such cases it is important simply to follow God's leading.

According to Luke and Mark, the little girl was not yet dead when Jairus made his first approach to Jesus, and at that point the synagogue ruler still had enough faith to believe that Jesus would heal her. In the delay caused by the need to heal the woman with the haemorrhage, however, she passed away. This upped the stakes. It took a lot more faith to believe that the child would be brought back from the dead; but Jesus, with grace and tenderness, and awesome authority, told him not to be afraid but only believe.

Then they went to the house, Jesus taking along with him Peter, James and John. He did not take with him Andrew, Peter's brother, and he would also leave Andrew out of the ascent of the mountain in Mark 9. No doubt the gifts of the three he did take with him made them the most appropriate companions at the time, and perhaps their rate of growth to spiritual maturity might also have had something to do with it. Many a modern elder or minister would have included Andrew so as not to upset him, but Jesus' love is tough, and he does not let such considerations dictate his choice of helper.

Although Mark's and Matthew's accounts could leave open the possibility that the girl was not actually dead, but perhaps in a coma or a trance, Luke makes it clear that the mourners knew that she was dead. Jesus, however, took her by the hand, and Mark quotes his exact words in Aramaic: *Talitha cumi:* words so tender that they sound almost onomatopoeic. They mean something like 'Come on, sweetheart, up you get.'

This story of a highly unlikely event, yet with a ring of truth, ends the great series of four remarkable miracles, a series which begins with a storm at sea, and ends with Jesus tenderly taking a dead twelve-year-old by the hand and bringing her back to life. Jesus is shown to be at one and the same time all-powerful and all-loving (see Psalm 62:11). Jairus and his wife are told to tell nobody, but that was a request they were unlikely to comply with! Matthew says that the news spread throughout that region, and the fact that we know the name of the synagogue ruler, does indeed suggest that it became widely known, and could be checked out.

9 The Syro-Phoenician Girl
(Matt. 15:21-28; Mark 7:24-30)

This miracle occurs on Gentile territory, Tyre, to which Jesus retreats before he commences his long march to Jerusalem to face his inevitable death. But his presence cannot be kept a secret, and a local Gentile woman makes something of a nuisance of herself in an attempt to get Jesus to heal her seriously disturbed daughter.

Jesus appears to treat her in an offhand way. His mission is to the Jewish people. He has not yet won them over to discipleship, and a move on Gentile territory is certainly not indicated. He knows that if he begins to perform healings here, the news will get around and he will find himself ministering willy-nilly. He tells the woman, 'It is not right to take the children's bread and toss it to "puppies"' (*kunaria*), not 'dogs', which is a much less gentle word. She replies, 'Yes, Lord, but even the puppies eat the crumbs that fall from their master's table.' The clever reply shows wisdom, and an understanding of whom Jesus is (whether we are children or puppies, he is still our master), and also trust that Jesus in his grace will meet her need. So she clearly has faith; and Jesus assures her that the demon has left her daughter. Matthew underlines the fact that the demon left her 'that very hour'.

This is the first example we have so far encountered of what the Germans call '*fernheilungen*' (distance healings). Such healings are widely reported in healing literature and give the lie to the idea that Jesus' healings were simply due to the impact of his personality on the people whom he encountered. Whatever this impact is supposed to have been, 'suggestion' or whatever, it cannot have worked on someone who was not there at the time!

Fernheilungen are widely reported, and also form part of my own experience. Some years ago, when I was preaching at a little Methodist chapel in rural Lancashire, I was invited by the leaders of the ongregation to join them afterwards at an evangelistic open-air meeting at a local caravan park. I went along with them, and we stood to sing and preach at what I felt was a rather unsuitable venue, where few people were likely to stop and listen. However, one solitary woman did come, and stood throughout the meeting at a distance, listening respectfully. When the meeting was over, she came across and spoke to us, and it emerged that when the meeting was held on a previous occasion she had plucked up the courage to ask the Methodists if they would pray for her sister who was seriously ill in hospital. Of course they did so, and now she had come to tell them that her sister had begun to feel very much better at the precise time that they had prayed for her.

10 A Deaf and Dumb Man
(Mark 7:31-37)

'Dumb' is something of an inaccurate description of this man's condition. The Greek word means that he spoke with difficulty.

The sufferer is brought to Jesus by others, a reminder that it is not always the sufferer's faith that connects with the healing power of Jesus. It may be the faith of friends or loved ones. As with Jairus, however (see earlier), they try to prescribe what Jesus should do: lay hands on him. In the event, Jesus once again does not do what he is asked to do, but what he knows is right, and he does something different – very different, as it turns out. He takes the man away privately, which is in contrast to his normally public healings, and a reminder to Christians with a very 'public' healing ministry that healings in public are not always appropriate. Why Jesus used the somewhat distasteful method of healing the man with spittle (which may explain why the other gospels omit the story) and

why he sighed, we do not know; but it certainly indicates:
- That nobody could have invented the story.
- That just as medicine sometimes uses distasteful methods (there being few things more distasteful than a surgical operation), so God sometimes uses distasteful methods to bring about healing by spiritual means; and
- Jesus came afresh to each new request for healing. There was no mass laying on of hands. Instead, he dealt with each person differently, as the Holy Spirit guided.

The people's reaction to the news of this healing was to proclaim, 'He has done everything well' (v37). This recalls the refrain in the Genesis story of the Creation of the World: 'God saw that it was good,' and probably is meant to do so. God creates; but God also re-creates. This is what he is doing in Jesus' healing ministry.

11 The Blind Man of Bethsaida
(Mark 8:22-26)

The location in a particular place, Bethsaida, a little town not far from Capernaum on the north side of the Sea of Galilee, tells to some degree in favour of the story's authenticity. On the other hand, the healing does bear some resemblances to the previous story of the deaf and dumb man. Each person is taken away privately, and in both cases spittle is used. There are three possible conclusions you could draw:
- The two stories are alternative versions of the same story (although there are also too many differences to make this theory plausible).
- Some of the features of one story have got attached to the other.
- It is recorded because that was how it was. (Bear in mind that Jesus used spittle elsewhere [John 9:6].)

Also in favour of the last point is the man's utterance in verse 24. The healing is not instantaneous, for miraculous healings are not always, not even for Jesus, and part of the way through the healing process, Jesus asks him, 'Do you see anything?' His reply could scarcely have been made up: 'I see people. They look like trees walking around.'

This will be enough to convince many people of the story's authenticity.

12 The 'Epileptic' Boy
(Matt. 17:14-18; Mark 9:14-27; Luke 9:38-43)

Some years ago I sat in a beautiful monastery garden on the edge of the Scottish Highlands drinking in the tranquillity of the setting. We were approaching the close of a Church Retreat which had turned out to be a blessing to many, a 'mountain-top experience', in fact. I was at peace. But then within two or three hours I was on the road, driving hard up to the north-east of Scotland to get to a certain church in time to take evening worship. I arrived with three minutes to spare, only to be told as I went in to the church that a dear friend and member of that congregation had just died, aged 45. I had come down from the mountain top and landed rather heavily.

'Mountain-top experiences' can be like that. Moses came down from Mount Sinai, where he had received the Ten Commandments, to find his people committing idolatry with a golden calf Aaron had made (Exodus 32). It is also true of this story. Peter, James and John had been up a mountain with Jesus – either Mount Hermon in the far north of the Holy Land, or more probably the much lower but prominent Mount Tabor in Galilee, and there Jesus had appeared 'transfigured' before them. It had been an extraordinary experience of the presence of God. When they came down from the mountain, 'they *saw*', according to Mark – and it is an eye-witness touch, as if Mark had heard the story from Peter – a large crowd around the other disciples, who were at their wits' end because they had with them a demonised boy and could not deliver him. Matthew, but not the other two, says that the boy was 'epileptic', and his symptoms certainly resemble epilepsy, but Jesus treats it as a rather extreme case of demonisation. Matthew is perhaps just describing the symptoms. At any rate, it is wrong to use this story as justification for assuming that people who suffer from epilepsy are possessed by demons. Whatever the diagnosis, this was a severely disturbed young man, and the disciples felt wretched in their powerlessness. Many of us have been there! To make matters worse, teachers of the Law were there, too, arguing about it. It resembles too closely for comfort a picture of the Western Christian Church on a bad day: youth disturbed, church leadership powerless to do anything about it, theologians arguing about it.

The people turn and see Jesus, who, according to Mark, still has on him the glow of the glory of the Lord, as had Moses when he came down from Mount Sinai. The father of the disturbed boy emerges from the crowd and approaches Jesus. '*Kyrie eleison,*' he says, according to Matthew: 'Lord, have mercy.' This is the first time the words occur in Christian literature. The father explains the desperate situation to Jesus and says, 'If you can, have pity on us and help us.' He does not hold out a lot of hope and is not strong in faith right then. Jesus quotes his words back at him: 'If you can.' Jesus points out that all things are possible to those who believe. The man's famous response is one many have often echoed: 'Lord, I believe. Help my unbelief.' But when we ask that of God, he *will* help our unbelief, for faith is itself a gift of God. Jesus then casts out the demon and gives the boy back to his father. The man's anguished cry to the Lord was all the faith that was needed. The same will often be true for us.

According to Mark and Matthew there is a 'post-mortem' afterwards. Jesus' relationship with his disciples was in important respects like that of a master-craftsman with apprentices. First he works by himself, then he works with them, watching, then they work with him, watching, then, after the Holy Spirit has been poured out on them, they carry out the Lord's work without his physical presence. In the course of this learning process, problems arise, but Jesus is lovingly approachable, and they ask him about them. 'Why couldn't we drive it out?' they say. Jesus' reply is worth remembering: 'This kind can come out only by prayer' (Mark 9:29).

The late John Wimber had a powerful healing ministry. One of my most vivid memories of him is of a huge concert hall full of people, hundreds of them in tears or calling out in anguish of soul, and all this after quite a dry lecture and no whipping up of emotion or manipulation that one could see, and Wimber on stage saying, 'Break their hearts, Lord.' Wimber's style was much imitated but usually without the results of that power. His wife Carol wrote a frank, raw biography of her husband after his death, which makes it clear what utter sacrifice and deep spirituality lay behind such a ministry. He once walked out of a meeting in deep distress when a talk that he had given was applauded. Jesus makes it clear that when you are dealing with very serious human need healing may come only through deep spirituality, self-discipline and sacrifice.

13 Blind Bartimaeus
(Matthew 20:29-34; Mark 10:46-52; Luke 18:35-43)

Scholars differ regarding the authenticity of this story. Dibelius and Bultmann (famous names in biblical scholarship in the early twentieth century) dismissed it as legendary. Vincent Taylor, however, thought the complete opposite. Anyone opting for the legend theory would need to come to terms with why the man was given a fairly ordinary name. A name and a location tend to imply that the story originated in historical fact, and it might have been a story cherished in later years by the Christian community in Jericho.

There are one or two small problems with the story. Matthew says there were two blind men, and gives no names. In his gospel we encountered two demoniacs in Gerasa as well, where Mark and Luke had only the one. All we can say is that at our present state of knowledge no explanation for this discrepancy is available. Another small problem is that while Mark and Matthew agree in placing the incident as Jesus left Jericho, Luke places it as he entered the town. A possible explanation is that there was an old part of Jericho and a new town, and Jesus would have passed through one to get to the other. It depends on what one thought of as Jericho proper, whether Jesus was entering or leaving it. However, the only way this problem matters is that if Jesus was leaving Jericho altogether, then it emphasises the fact that this was Bartimaeus' last chance to get out of the prison of his blindness.

Whatever conclusion we reach about the problem, it remains true that Bartimaeus was urgently seizing an opportunity. It is probable that Jesus, then on his last journey to Jerusalem, would never pass that way again. Bartimaeus might not have known that he would never return, but would still not have rated his chances of encountering Jesus again very highly. He therefore seized the opportunity, calling out, 'Jesus, Son of David, have mercy on me!'

The beggar might have been blind physically but he was certainly not spiritually blind. The expression 'Son of David' is obviously a title of the Messiah, and it is interesting that the rest of the crowd do not use the expression. For them it is 'Jesus of Nazareth' who is passing by. 'Son of David' occurs ten times in Matthew's gospel, more than three times as often as it occurs in any of the others. In Matthew its use is cumulative. It is as if we see people gradually grasping who Jesus is, and we move through 'Could this be the Son of David?' (12:23) to the chanting of the crowds as they laid palms at Jesus' feet the Sunday before he died: 'Hosanna to the Son of David' (21:9). Matthew's gospel is very Jewish, and he is concerned to demonstrate that Jesus is indeed the Messiah, the Son of David, the object of the Jewish people's hopes and longings. Bartimaeus saw with the eye of faith who Jesus was, and that insight, along with his action of calling upon Jesus, constituted the faith that healed him.

What about the message for us? In the Depression years

of the 1920s and 1930s, little groups of out-of-work merchant seamen could often be seen waiting by the lock gates at Port Talbot in South Wales as tramp steamers locked out of the docks to put to sea. They would wait in the hope that a short-handed ship would come through the locks and they might be able to hop aboard and join the crew. Sometimes there was indeed a place vacant for a lucky seaman. 'The pier head jump', as it was called, is a parable of our seeking God. Although God is always around, and his arms, as it were, are always open to welcome sinful and needy people, there are times in our lives when 'the iron is hot'; a God-opportunity has come along and we may never be so close to God or so strongly motivated to take the step of faith again. Jesus of Nazareth is passing by. We must seize the moment.

14 The Centurion's Servant
(Matt. 8:5-13; Luke 7:1-10)

We have come to the end of Mark's miracle stories, and turn now to the only miracle story found in 'Q' (common to Matthew and Luke, but not found in Mark). There are quite big differences between the two stories. Matthew does his usual abridgement, which involves leaving out the little delegation coming to Jesus, but he does add a saying of Jesus:

'I tell you the truth, I have not found anyone in Israel with such great faith. I say to you that many will come from the east and the west, and will take their places at the feast with Abraham, Isaac and Jacob in the kingdom of heaven. But the subjects of the kingdom will be thrown outside, into the darkness, where there will be weeping and gnashing of teeth' (vv10-12).

By including this, the Jew Matthew expresses his heartbroken concern that his own people are rejecting their Messiah. He may have been writing after the Roman armies destroyed Jerusalem in AD70, and in the recognition that had the Jewish nation and Jewish authorities accepted Jesus for whom he was, the whole spiritual and political climate of Jerusalem would have been so different that the siege and destruction of the city would not have occurred. So Matthew's version of the story undoubtedly has a particular slant to it. Luke's approach is quite different. As a Gentile, he perhaps could not have got away with including such a saying at this point. Were he to have done so, he certainly would have left himself open to the charge of anti-Semitism. Matthew, writing as a Jew, is quoting his Master out of grief, not out of hate or prejudice. But it does mean that Luke's account has a kindlier tone.

Some commentators suggest that the centurion may not have been a Roman. There were no Roman forces in Galilee prior to AD44. Hence he may have been a member of King Antipas's soldiery, who modelled themselves on Roman military organisation. The point is, he was a Gentile. Luke tells of a little delegation approaching Jesus on the centurion's behalf and explaining that he was worthy to have Jesus do this for him because he loved their nation and had built their synagogue. The man himself emerges as what Oliver Cromwell would have called 'a plain russet-coated captain': straightforward, down-to-earth, no nonsense, wholesome, and yet perceptive too. Jesus has already decided to go to the centurion's house (in something of a contrast to Elisha, who in the story referred to in the Introduction to this book would not even come out of his house to minister to a foreign military officer!), but the centurion (directly in Matthew, via a messenger in Luke) tells Jesus that he is not worthy to have him come under his roof, but he has only to say the word and his servant will be healed, because he is also a man with authority and he says to one man 'Go' and he goes, and to another man 'Come' and he comes. Once again, the words have a ring of truth, and are not the sort of thing likely to have been invented. The centurion displays for our benefit the kind of faith that is required when a miracle is needed: a God-given ability to trust the authority of Jesus in a quite specific situation.

William Hendriksen, writing of the centurion, speaks of 'a combination in one person of a love so affectionate, a consideration so thoughtful, an insight so penetrating, a humility so outstanding and a trust so unlimited.' On the strength of this, another 'distance healing' takes place.

15 The Two Blind Men
(Matthew 9:27-31)

For the significance of the term 'Son of David' refer back to the comments on the healing of Bartimaeus.

Once again in Matthew, two sufferers from the same thing are healed at once, and we have already seen that no explanation for Matthew's preference for pairs is available. It is possible, though, that the two blind men took fire from one another, and boosted one another's faith. It is far harder to have faith when you are alone with no one around to confirm or corroborate it, than it is when you have the company of someone who shares your faith and can encourage it. So when Jesus asked them if they believed that he was able to do what they asked, they unhesitatingly replied, 'Yes, Lord.' A helpful comment on the incident is Matthew 18:19, 20:

'I tell you that if two of you on earth agree about anything you ask for, it will be done for you by my Father in heaven. For where two or three come together in my name, there am I with them.'

Jesus asks them what they want, which is not necessarily his usual practice; and this time he touches their eyes. He does not simply command healing; and if he used spittle, Matthew doesn't mention it. Once again, note the flexibility of his approach. Once again, too, he sternly charges secrecy, and once again the healed persons take no notice whatsoever.

16 The Dumb Demoniac
(Matt. 9:32-34; Luke 11:14)

This is an intriguing instance of a physical condition being brought on by demonisation. There are elements in the Church of today, particularly in the developing world, who would want to attribute most illness to demons, and would no doubt use this text in support of their beliefs. Such people need to balance this text with Mark 7:31-37, where a deaf and dumb man is healed but demonisation is not involved.

The man's deliverance gets two significantly different reactions. The crowd are amazed. 'Nothing like this has ever been seen in Israel,' they say. The Pharisees, however, are far from happy about Jesus' message, but have to find some explanation for his obvious success as a healer and exorcist. So they claim that he drives out demons by the prince of demons. Jesus, of course, had replied to that charge elsewhere when he said, 'How can Satan cast out Satan?'

Notice also that the Pharisees' explanation is evidence that Jesus did exorcisms and that they were effective. If his exorcisms had been ineffective, they would have needed only to point that out, but they couldn't, for people were being effectively set free. Therefore the only card that the Pharisees had left to play was the far-fetched accusation that it was by the prince of demons that Jesus did his exorcisms.

Miraculous events do polarise opinion. In many societies, and many individuals, remarkable events in response to prayer can trigger faith, but we need to be aware that they can have the opposite effect. People witnessing wonders can become fearful and angry that their world has been disturbingly invaded, and therefore react badly. And this can happen in very religious circles, whether Jewish, Islamic, or, for that matter, Christian.

17 The Blind and Dumb Demoniac
(Matthew 12:22)

This little story is rather similar to the story of the healing of the dumb demoniac in Matthew 9:32-34. Like that story (which some would claim to be another version of the same story) it evokes a polarised reaction among the witnesses.

Some people are deeply impressed, and are beginning to come round to the idea that this might be the Son of David, the Messiah; others go completely the opposite way. Jesus is not good, but evil, and he does miracles, they say, because he is in league with the prince of demons.

Jesus, who was not always meek and mild, gives a scorching defence of his position in the verses that follow (12:25-37). How, he says, can Satan drive out Satan? It would wreck Satan's cause. It is illogical to think that he would cast demons out. Jesus says that what he is doing is tying up 'the strong man' so that he can rob his house of all the people he has damaged. He also sternly warns his opponents that they are in danger of calling good evil and thereby blaspheming against the Holy Spirit. The central verse of his defence is verse 28: 'If I drive out demons by the Spirit of God, then the kingdom of God has come upon you.' (See also the Byway on Demons and Deliverance.)

Doctor Luke

The Man

It is not known for certain where Luke came from. A tradition was passed down in the early Christian Church that he hailed from Antioch: not the great city situated on the coast of what is now Syria, but Pisidian Antioch, in the interior of what is now Turkey. There is also a theory that he lived in Philippi, at the head of the Aegean Sea, but the only evidence for it is that the 'we-passages' commence in Acts 16 at Philippi. There is also a tradition that he never married, and died at the ripe old age of 84 in a country called Boeotia.

Traditions are sometimes correct, sometimes not. We do know from Colossians 4:14 that Luke was a

doctor, because Paul calls him 'beloved physician'. And we also know that he was not a Jew, because in the same epistle (4:11) Paul mentions three men who, he says, are the only Jews among his fellow-workers. Luke's name is not among them, so we conclude that he was a Gentile.

Luke was, nevertheless, a close companion of Paul. The 'we-passages' of the book of Acts (if we assume that he was indeed the author of that book) suggest a faithful follower, and a great admirer, of Paul. Colossians bears this out, as does 2 Timothy 4:11 ('only Luke is with me now') and also Philemon 24.

The Gospel of Luke and the book of Acts of the Apostles form a two-volume work attributed to him. It was common in biblical times for books to be attributed to eminent figures who did not actually write them, so we cannot just assume that Luke wrote both of these books without a brief look at the evidence, which is as follows:

- Luke writes courteous, learned-sounding prologues to both books, and they read just like the prologues with which learned authors, particularly doctors such as Galen, would commence their works.
- He avoids using popular terms for 'illness' and illnesses. *Malakia*, a popular term, is used three times for illness in Matthew, never in Luke.
- He uses medical terms as metaphors. When Paul and Barnabas fell out (Acts 15:39, 40) Luke says there arose a 'paroxysm' between them, and in describing the storm and shipwreck, he says in Acts 27:17 that the sailors 'bound up the ship with bandages'. Where Mark uses the popular term for an illness, Luke replaces it with the correct medical term. And when Paul strikes Elymas the sorcerer blind

(Acts 13:11) the word he uses of the blindness is the same word that Galen the famous physician uses for 'cataract'. He uses the correct term for 'paralytic' replacing Mark's words for it in Mark 2:10. There are many examples of this sort of thing throughout both Luke's Gospel and Acts, and they are consistent with Luke the physician's being the author.

• Luke was not a famous apostle, so there would be no particular reason for attributing his books to him if he was not, in fact, their author.

His Medicine

Luke might actually have been a slave, or a freed slave, because doctors often were, an idea which seems strange to us, though slaves in those times could carry considerable authority and responsibility. But what kind of medicine did he practise?

In the fifth century BCE a man from the Island of Cos, called Hippocrates, who was an 'Asclepiad', i.e. a temple servant at the Temple of Asclepiades the god of healing, began to adopt a philosophical and scientific approach to the subject. He carefully studied patterns of symptoms and developed a theory of four 'humours', namely, Blood, Phlegm, Yellow Bile and Black Bile, which he claimed needed to be in balance if health was to be maintained. The school of medicine which he founded was called the 'Dogmatists', and schools of this type of medicine grew up in many places, including Alexandria, Smyrna, Ephesus, and, interestingly, Tarsus, Paul's home town. One of the teachers in Alexandria was Herophilus (c.330-260 BCE), who performed vivisection on condemned criminals and was therefore termed 'the butcher' by the Christian writer Tertullian.

One of his pupils founded another school of thought called the 'Empiricists', who discarded the current dogmas in favour of observation and experiment.

It was about that time that Medicine was divided into three branches: Surgery, Pharmacy, and Dietetics. Then other schools grew out of that one in turn, such as the 'Methodics', who taught that the body was made up of atoms with spaces between them, which sounds to us astonishingly modern; but then they went on to say that to maintain health, the spaces between the atoms should be neither too wide nor too narrow! Stoic philosophers said that the world had a soul or 'pneuma', and health consisted in being in right relationship to it. The head of the school of medicine that corresponded to it was Athenaeus, and his followers were called 'Pneumatics'. Finally, the 'Eclectics' sought to pick up the best ideas from all the other schools.

Luke's training would have been in one of these schools, which obviously anticipated some of the ideas of modern medicine, even if in other respects they were dangerously wide of the mark. Which school Luke was of, we have no way of knowing, and neither do we know to what extent he allowed his ideas to be modified after he became a Christian.

His Importance

Luke is important not only because he wrote two books, but also because, as Church historian Harnack wrote: He protected his science, medicine, in the Church, and triumphantly averted for the Christian Church the consequences of a Christianity shunning nature.

18 The Widow's Son
(Luke 7:11-17)

If you were to discount for a while the question of whether miracles can happen, and run a 'likelihood assessment' on this story, it would actually score quite highly. Nain, at the foot of the imposing Mount Tabor in Galilee, is not a place mentioned elsewhere in Scripture, and has no religious significance, which means that anyone inventing the story or embroidering it as it was passed on would be seriously unlikely to locate it there. This counts for the story's authenticity. So does the fact that archaeologists have discovered tombs at Nain, and so too the archaic language. There are still signs in the Greek that the story was told in Aramaic at first (see Introduction), and for the scholar this is a sign that the story is of early origin. Yet this story with many marks of authenticity is about a raising from the dead!

The passage is very much the kind of story Luke loved to tell. He alone tells the story, so it belongs to the 'L material' (See Byway on Differences between the Gospels). Out of the fifty-five L stories and sayings, seventeen involve women. Luke's compassionate heart and concern for outsiders – for that is what women were in that society – made him particularly interested in Jesus' attitude towards them; and he would, of course, have been particularly concerned about a woman who had lost her husband and then her only son. There would have been unbearable grief and a future of loneliness and poverty for her, if Jesus had not intervened. This is classic miracle territory: someone is utterly at the end of her tether, then God steps in.

The people respond warmly, and assume that Jesus is a great prophet; but this is early in his ministry, and they have yet to 'cotton on' to the possibility that he might be the Messiah.

We do not normally associate a miracle like this with our own times. Healings can be coped with. Raisings from the dead are an entirely different matter! Yet stories of raisings from the dead, sometimes well authenticated, are not unknown in contemporary Christianity. Revd Tom Stuckey spoke some years ago of a conversation he had with a Greek Orthodox research student at Edinburgh University. When asked what his research was about, the man explained that he was studying accounts of raisings from the dead. Somewhat taken aback, Stuckey said, 'You mean there are some?' 'Oh, yes,' was the reply. 'Quite a lot, actually.'

19 Mary Magdalene
(Luke 8:2)

This is hardly a story, merely a reference to the healing of Mary (and, incidentally, evidence that Jesus' exorcisms did have a lasting effect). It occurs in the midst of a list of names of female disciples of Jesus, and Jesus is said to have cast seven demons out of her.

Mary Magdalene is so called because she came from the town of Magdala, near the shores of the Sea of Galilee between Capernaum and Tiberias. Some Bible scholars believe her to have been a different Mary from the one who lived with her sister Martha in Bethany. Others point out that Luke provides no linkage with the sinful woman whose anointing of Jesus is described in the previous chapter (vv36-38). If she was the same person, they argue, Luke would have made the connection. The reference to seven devils indicates that she had been a seriously disturbed person, but that does not necessarily imply that her former life had been immoral. At the same time, she does seem to have been comfortably off financially, because Luke tells us that 'these women were helping to support the disciples out of their own means'. One of the others was Joanna, wife of Herod's steward Chuza, no less, who must certainly have been a woman of means. It can be deduced that Mary had wealth too, but she had not had mental stability until Jesus stepped into her life.

In the wake of the incident in the previous chapter concerning Jesus' anointing by a sinful woman, Jesus told a parable in answer to his host's disapproval of the woman's behaviour (7:40-47), the point of which is that if you have been forgiven little then you do not love very much, and if you have been forgiven much, then you love much. Something similar surely applied to Mary's healing. If we have been healed from something very serious, and now look out on a future of infinite hope and possibility with eyes of serenity and normality where once there had been darkness, mental pain and horror, then we shall love the one who healed us very much.

With the healing there must also have come to Mary a feeling of being affirmed. Women were marginalised in that society and largely excluded from public life. Jesus' attitude rendered that obsolete. As an old hymn says, Jesus 'crowned women with an honour never known before'. It is not surprising, therefore, that Mary appears to have developed a close relationship with Jesus, with the result that she was the first person to whom Jesus appeared after he had risen from the dead (John 20:10-18).

20 The Bent Woman
(Luke 13:10-13)

Sometimes, otherwise excellent translations of the Bible give misleading impressions of what the original Greek text said, and I have, as it were, to swallow hard and say that I think this is the case here. The New International Version says this woman, bent double, had been 'crippled by a spirit' for eighteen years, but what the Greek actually says is 'she had a spirit of infirmity'. I mention this because the woman is usually regarded by commentators as being demonised, and Jesus' healing of her is usually thought to have been an exorcism. I want strongly to suggest that that was not the case.

In no other case in the Bible are hands laid on a demoniac, as they are here. I have even spoken to people who reckon to have some experience of deliverance ministry today, who told me that they would never lay hands on a demoniac because it would have unfortunate consequences, though they did not specify what those consequences would be! Also, there is no command to 'come out', as there is in most of the other cases, and no commotion made by the demon. The language used about the woman's condition is different, too. In all the other cases of exorcism described in the gospels the sufferer is said to have a demon or an unclean spirit, or to be 'demonised'. The term used here is more reminiscent of Paul's language when he wrote to the Corinthians, 'Shall I come to you with a whip, or in love and *with a gentle spirit?*' (1 Corinthians 4:21), or in Galatians 6:1, where the term crops up again. Paul did not mean being possessed by a spirit called 'Gentleness' or a spirit who happened to be gentle; he simply meant an *attitude* of gentleness.

I believe that the expression 'spirit of infirmity' is Dr Luke's way of saying that the woman's physical symptoms had a psychological origin. Mental states can have bodily effects, whether through psychosomatic conditions or through hysteria. In fact it is a basic insight of the ministry of healing that mind and body are closely connected. Mental states can result from physical conditions, and physical conditions from mental states. It looks as if the latter was what had happened here.

This being the case, it may look as though the story provides ammunition for that school of thought which would put down most of Jesus' healings to psychological causes. However, Dr John Wilkinson told me in an interview that even if the woman's condition had a psychological origin, being bent double for eighteen years would have resulted in serious structural damage to the spine, and, however deep the psychological healing, she still would not have been able to stand up without physical healing.

Jesus does say that Satan had bound the woman, and these words may suggest that this was an exorcism after all, but we need to remember that Luke stressed how sickness belonged to the realm of evil, from which Jesus had come to set us free. It is interesting, too, that Paul's much-discussed 'thorn in the flesh' of 2 Corinthians 12:7, which is considered in a later section, could have been a chronic illness, and he called it 'a messenger of Satan'.

The story is very much Luke. It is about a woman. There is a doctor's interest in what caused her condition. There is a gentleness, too, and a wonderful affirmation of the woman in Jesus' reference to her as 'a daughter of Abraham'. Zacchaeus, now a saved and reformed character, is described as 'a son of Abraham' in Luke 19:9. This is surely Jesus' way of saying, 'You are not an outsider anymore. You *belong.*' Such affirmation is often an important part of the healing process.

21 The Man with Dropsy
(Luke 14:1-4)

Here Luke displays some discernible organisation, because the healing which takes place at a banquet forms part of a chapter of 'banquets'. The account of the healing is brief indeed, and is swallowed up in a controversy about healing on the Sabbath. The story exposes the absurdity and cruelty of a 'legalistic' morality, which can be 'nit-picking' over the details of human behaviour yet completely overlook caring, love, justice, and even, sometimes, common-sense. Legalism is not simply a Jewish problem, for it has affected Christianity throughout its history. For instance, in the reign of James VI of Scotland, two feuding clans in south-west Scotland lined up to fight one another, but then dispersed for a day because it was Sunday, returning on Monday to pick up the fight where they had left off! It is this kind of moral blindness to which legalism leads, and it was the same mentality which questioned Jesus' right to heal on the Sabbath. Saying all this may appear to be taking us into a different area from healing, but not entirely, because legalism can help to create a whole atmosphere in which the Holy Spirit is not allowed to do what he wants to do.

22 Ten Leprosy cases
(Luke 17:11-17)

See the discussion of the healing of leprosy (healing number 3 above) for information about the disease. Luke gives us a geographical location here. Jesus was travelling on the borders of Galilee and Samaria, Samaria being a land inhabited by a people of partial non-Jewish origin who were unorthodox in their religion and were viewed with distaste or even hatred by the Jews. That was the point of Jesus' parable of the Good Samaritan. Luke probably says this only to explain how it came about that one of the ten healed was a Samaritan.

There are a couple of lessons to be learnt from this story of the gratitude of the one and the ingratitude of the nine:

• Once you have been healed, however it happened, medically or otherwise, the right response is praise and thanksgiving. To 'let the joy out' is not to lose the joy, but to reinforce it. I wonder if the ungrateful men lost their healing in the long run?

• When we help the needy and the outcast we are inclined, if we lack experience, to expect that they will appreciate the help they have been given and will show it. It is wonderful when they do, but all too often they do not. Perhaps they think that because life has dealt them a bad deal, the help that you have given them is no more than their due. Whether or not this is the case, their attitude will always cause pain, but it is something we need to be prepared for, because even Jesus experienced it.

23 Malchus's Ear
(Luke 22:50, 51)

This, the fifth and last of the healing miracles peculiar to Luke, occurs in the strangest of settings, the Garden of Gethsemane at the moment of Jesus' arrest. According to Luke alone, just before they departed from the upper room in Jerusalem where they had eaten their last supper together, Jesus said to them:

'But now if you have a purse, take it, and also a bag; and if you don't have a sword, sell your cloak and buy one. It is written: "And he was numbered with the transgressors"; and I tell you that this must be fulfilled in me. Yes, what is written about me is reaching its fulfilment.'

'The disciples said, "See, Lord, here are two swords."
' "That is enough," he replied' (22:36-38).

What Jesus meant by the references to swords is not clear. However, it has been helpfully suggested that the meaning is that once the 'Shepherd' had been taken, the sheep would be scattered, and, in becoming fugitives, they would need among other things swords to defend themselves – from wild beasts, not people.

In the event, they seem to have picked him up the wrong way, as they often did; and when the posse came to arrest Jesus, one of the disciples actually struck the high priest's servant who was there, cutting off his ear. Only John (18:10) tells us that the assailant was Simon Peter. The other gospel writers all relate the incident, but, perhaps out of respect, fail to mention who did it. It is also John alone, who often seems to have inside information, who tells us that the servant's name was Malchus.

In all the gospels Jesus makes it quite clear that the wounding was well out of order. In fact, in Matthew 26:52 he is recorded as saying, 'Put your sword back into its place, for all who draw the sword will die by the sword.'

It is only Luke, however, who tells us that Jesus there and then healed the man's ear, a healing remarkable not only for its setting and the complete lack of faith involved, but also for the degree of organic damage which would have needed repairing.

The story's authenticity has often been questioned, on the grounds that the other three gospels would surely have mentioned such a remarkable thing if it were true. There could, however, be an explanation of which we are unaware. It

remains a powerful story, with certain important lessons:
- Christian purposes are rarely, if ever, achieved by violence.
- It is a remarkable indication of the grace of Jesus (his 'undeserved love', for that is what 'grace' means), that he should so wonderfully heal someone who had, after all, come to help drag him away to be tortured to death.
- The servant was wounded as a result of misplaced zeal on the part of a disciple. Christians today are rarely guilty of wounding one another with weapons, but they can wound one another with words or other acts and do serious emotional or spiritual damage in their misplaced zeal. In the course of my own ministry, I have come across a number of people who have been quite seriously damaged by such wrong words or misplaced 'ministry'. Zealous disciples wound. Christ heals.

Health in John's Gospel

We are now about to enter John's gospel for the first time, but, before we do, there are certain things to note about John. He does have things to say that are both unique and essential.

Dr Frank Lake, a leading light in the Christian ministry of healing in the latter half of the twentieth century, was in Vellore, India, in 1950, designing training programmes for psychiatry students, and had become frustrated because he found himself unable to define what could be described as 'normality'. At that time he met a distinguished Swiss theologian called Emil Brunner, who was teaching in India, and shared his perplexity with him. Brunner responded by directing him to John's gospel; and this was a revelation for Lake. John's gospel tells of spiritual rebirth (3:3, 5-7), of 'living water' which does not leave you dissatisfied, like so many of the

> other means of fulfilment on offer (John 4:10-15), and of 'more abundant life' (John 10:10).
>
> All of us seek real living, rather than mere existence, and John's gospel makes it clearer than anywhere else in the New Testament that this real life, characterised by meaning, fulfilment and joy, a kind of inner *shalom* if you like, is to be found in Jesus.

24 The Nobleman's Son
(John 4:46-54)

The story before us is the second of the six big miracle stories in John, which he calls 'signs'. These stories can be divided up into two groups of three, each beginning with what would usually be termed a nature miracle. The series as a whole begins with the almost light-hearted story of Jesus' turning water into wine at a wedding in Cana of Galilee (John 2:1-11), and ends with the staggering miracle of the raising of Mary and Martha's brother Lazarus from the dead (John 11).

This story bears some resemblance to the healing of the centurion's servant, suggesting that this may be John's version of that story. After all, they both involve an important personage based in Capernaum, and both involve a 'distance healing'. At the same time, there are major differences, and it is on this basis that we are visiting it separately from the other story.

We find Jesus back in Cana, where he turned the water into wine. The nobleman, or 'royal official', actually lived at Capernaum, but he came to Jesus at Cana, some miles away, and begged Jesus to heal his son. The Master's reply is, to us, puzzling. 'Unless you people see signs and wonders,' he says, 'you will never believe.' He may have been addressing the nobleman, but this is unlikely. The man was not testing him, as others did, by asking him repeatedly to do signs to confirm that what he was saying was true. He just wanted to see his loved one well. Jesus must surely have been addressing a more general audience; and he appears to be saying that people should not need miraculous signs to cause them to believe, for much later in John we find him saying to Thomas, 'Blessed are those who have not seen and yet have believed.' At the same time, though, he seems to be saying that if it takes signs and wonders to cause people to believe, then signs and wonders they shall have. A *fernheilung* (distance healing) then takes place.

25 The Lame Man at the Bethesda Pool
(John 5:1-16)

Pilgrims to Jerusalem can visit the site of this healing. In the middle decades of the twentieth century, there was a shift in scholarly attitudes to John's Gospel. There had been a tendency to regard his book as a reverent but fictitious set of stories about Jesus. In 1930, Kirsopp Lake felt able to write: 'John may contain a few fragments of true tradition, but in the main it is fiction.' C. H. Dodd, writing in 1963, was much less sceptical about the gospel. He felt that there were ancient and reliable traditions behind it. Archaeological discovery has helped to change attitudes, in particular the discovery of the site of this healing. Excavations were begun by the White Fathers in 1878 on a site 100 yards north of the Temple in Jerusalem. Those excavations, not completed until 1932, revealed a double pool with slightly different water levels, oblong in layout, with pillared walkways running around all four sides and a fifth between the two pools: the 'five porticoes'.

C. H. Dodd suggested that the story is full of symbolism. The five porticoes might suggest the five books of the law: Genesis, Exodus, Leviticus, Numbers and Deuteronomy. The sufferer could not be healed by the law, but only by the coming of the Kingdom of God in the Messiah, Jesus. This may be one meaning; the story is a 'sign', after all, and John appears to have loved to find symbolic significance in actual places or events, but the pool did exist, and this is evidence of the truth of the story, even if it cannot prove it.

There are many other points of interest about the passage.

❏ Jesus asks the man, 'Do you want to be healed?' It sounds like a silly question. The man might have been tempted to think, 'What does he think I've been doing here for the last thirty-eight years!'

My own feeling is that Jesus asked this question because deep down the man might not have truly wanted healing. His whole life would have been built around his illness and the adjustment needed after recovery would have been huge. Also, when you are ill you get a lot of attention, which will cease if you get well, and in addition you will have to work and pay your own way in the world if you recover! The man's subsequent contacts with the religious authorities suggest that he had neither the faith nor the attitude of the man born blind (John 9), which could suggest that he had the kind of personality which would cling to sickness.

❏ No faith seems to have been involved anywhere, either as a condition of healing or as a consequence of it.

❏ This is one of only two miracles where the sufferer's condition is associated with his own sin. We shall see that in the New Testament illness isn't necessarily a consequence of sin, though it can be; and it is here. The other case, interestingly enough, is that of the paralysed man let down through the roof (Mark 2:1-12), and in both cases the sufferer is told to rise, take up his bed and walk. It is as if Jesus is telling them that sin has no more hold over them: they can walk free.

❏ All this happens by a pool where a lot of sick people gather because a disturbance of the water surface, due no doubt to natural causes, occurs now and again and is believed to be caused by an angel. The first into the water at that point will be healed: a tricky manoeuvre if you're paralysed! Jesus totally ignores the pool, and one wonders what that has to say about healing springs like Lourdes or Walsingham.

❏ Although there would be sick people all around, it seems as if Jesus singled out this one man for treatment. Of course he might have healed many others at the same time and place, but the way the story is told seems to exclude that. We have to face the fact that Jesus might not invariably have miraculously healed sick people with whom he came in contact, and that miracles do not happen to order. Peter and John were released from prison by an angel (Acts 5:17-20); later on, Peter was released (Acts 12:5-10); and in Acts 16:23-33 Paul and Silas were miraculously sprung from jail. John the Baptist, however, was not. On what basis did Jesus heal one person, but not another? We do not have to look far for an answer, because later on, in John 5, verses 19-21 we are given a clue:

'I tell you the truth, the Son can do nothing by himself; he can do only what he sees his Father doing, because whatever the Father does the Son also does. For the Father loves the Son and shows him all he does. Yes, to your amazement he will show him even greater things than these. For just as the Father raises the dead and gives them life, even so the Son gives life to whom he is pleased to give it.'

These verses present us with a picture of Jesus receiving guidance from God as to when, where, how, and upon whom, miracles are to be performed. God in his wisdom knows best what should happen and what should not, and Jesus has such a relationship of closeness and love with his Father that he knows what God intends. The lesson for us is that, assuming that Jesus is our role model for the healing ministry, the person with such a ministry needs to cultivate a dedicated life, a deep spirituality and a closeness to God which will enable her (or him) to know what God intends to do in any particular case.

❏ There is an element of aftercare in the story. The healed man is of questionable character, and appears to remain like that even after he has met Jesus and been healed. (It can happen!) He even appears to have betrayed Jesus to the authorities (verse 15). Knowing what he is like, Jesus nevertheless cares enough to follow him up. He tracks him down to the temple, where hopefully, but not certainly, the man might have gone to give thanks, and tells him, 'Stop sinning or something worse may happen to you.' We can lose our healing through disobedience to God. It was after this warning that the man was able to identify Jesus to the authorities, and betray him. It is quite possible, though we are not told, that he lost his healing.

26 The Man Born Blind
(John 9:1-41)

The setting of this miracle was Jerusalem, probably at the time of the Jewish Feast of Tabernacles. The feast, in which the pilgrims built themselves little huts made out of branches and foliage, celebrated the grape harvest and commemorated the time when Israel lived in tents in the wilderness. Jerusalem was crowded and Jesus had had bruising confrontations and controversies with the Jewish authorities, which had amounted to a contest between light and darkness. In the course of the controversy, Jesus uttered the immortal words: 'I am the light.' Religion can go wrong, can promote a kind of moral blindness and become a vehicle for evil. This has been profoundly true of Christianity during various periods of history, and we still live with the shame of that. But let's visit this miracle and turn to the wider issues later.

As Jesus and the disciples pass by, they see a man born blind, a fact that they probably establish from conversation with him. This causes the disciples a big problem. Their understanding was the normal Jewish understanding of those times, that if you were sick it was because you had sinned, but if you had been born blind, how could you have had time to sin? So maybe it was his parents' sin that had caused the trouble.

Jesus replies that neither was the case, and in so doing he loosens the link between sin and sickness as a punishment. Sin and sickness *are* linked, it is true, because my sickness can be caused by my own sin, or someone else's sin against me, or it may indeed *sometimes* be God's punishment for sin, but the equation to be sick equals to be punished by sickness is incorrect. Jesus has some more words to say to this effect in Luke 13:2-4.

Jesus does, however, say that the blindness has a purpose: it is so that God's power will be displayed in this man's life. We have to conclude from this that sometimes, but not all the time, that is the role that sickness will play in a person's life. Jesus also says that there is a kind of urgency about doing good. He knows the powers of darkness are gathering, for he has just come away from an encounter with them. He knows that one day soon they will destroy him. When that happens there will be no more healings for a time, but meanwhile, while he is in the world, he repeats, 'I am the light of the world', a saying beloved of Christians for whom Christ has become their light. The Latin motto of my old theological college is *Lux Vita Caritas*: Light, Life, Love. It's a rather wonderful motto because it describes three major characteristics of the Christian life. There is a certain order about the three characteristics too. First we receive light, the light that makes John Masefield's character, Saul Kane, say, following his conversion, 'O glory of the lighted mind/how deaf I'd been, how dumb, how blind.'

Then having received *light* we discover we have entered new *life*, mentioned throughout John (see John 10:10) and a consequence of this is that we become able to *love* (John 13:34).

But we have strayed some distance from the teeming streets of Jerusalem, and the immediate need of the blind man. Jesus makes clay out of spittle and slaps it on the blind man's eyes! Spittle was used in healing in ancient times, but its use here may simply be symbolic. Jesus wants not only to do a healing but to make it a sign. The man's blindness represents something, the blindness of evil. The dirt representing the evil needs to be washed off. Jesus therefore sends the man to the pool of Siloam. This pool still exists, and John, who loves to find symbolism in actual places and events, points out that its name means 'sent'. The man goes to Siloam and the dirt is washed off and he can see. Perhaps John had in mind the waters of baptism, where the dirt of sin is washed off and our blindness is healed; we can now understand the truth; we can see the world's beauty instead of darkness; and we can see God's hand at work and experience his presence.

The consequences of the healing are, first of all, confusion about whether the healed man was the one who used to beg, or someone who looked like him – a life-like touch (see the Introduction). The man is taken to the Pharisees, and interviewed by them. He confesses that he believes Christ to be a prophet, which is also a life-like touch, because an embroidered story would have had him confessing that Jesus was the Messiah or the Son of God. The man's parents are sent for to confirm the healing but are afraid to comment on how it happened, because already the opposition to Jesus is such that to be a follower of Jesus means to be put out of the synagogue. In a second interview the man confesses, 'Whether he [Jesus] is a sinner or not, I don't know. One thing I do know. I was blind but now I see! . . . We know that God does not listen to sinners. He listens to the godly man who does his will. Nobody has ever heard of opening the eyes of a man born blind. If this man were not from God, he could do nothing.' Words that still have force for us today.

A friend of mine, who had himself considerable need for inner healing at one time, was sitting chatting on a train with a disabled person, and the conversation became rather deep. 'The difference between you and me,' said the disabled person, 'is that people can see my disability. They can't see yours.' The story condemns the moral and spiritual blindness of those who couldn't see the blind man's healing for the glorious thing that it was, and who should have known better.

27 The Raising of Lazarus
(John 11:1-44)

This, the longest miracle of the gospels, relates how Jesus called his friend Lazarus alive from the tomb where he was dead and buried. It is the last and most dramatic of John's six 'signs', and occurred not very long before Jesus' last trip to Jerusalem. Indeed, according to John, it triggered off the events that led to Jesus' death. Like all the other signs in John it points to a particular truth about Jesus, in this case that he is 'the Resurrection and the Life'.

There is a conversation with Lazarus's sister Martha, designed, it appears, to draw out her faith. When shown the tomb, 'Jesus wept' (verse 35, the shortest in the Bible), and the Jewish onlookers say, 'See how he loved him', but if Jesus knew what was about to happen – as verse 11 says he did – then the meaning of Jesus' tears was not so much grief over the loss of Lazarus as empathy with the grieving sisters Martha and Mary. This quality of being able to 'weep with them that weep' is an important qualification for the healer. Mahesh Chavda tells of years of preparation and caring for those in need before he began to be used in healing, which trained him in compassion. Jesus is 'deeply moved', but here again is that awkward word we encountered in the healing of the man with leprosy (miracle number 3), which usually means 'moved with anger'. Once again it seems inappropriate here, but the distinguished Aramaic scholar Matthew Black argues that the original Aramaic word used in telling the story would have meant 'deeply troubled'.

In verses 38 to 44 the narrative, a brilliant piece of story-telling, slows down, building tension, until Jesus calls out, 'Lazarus, come forth,' whereupon Lazarus comes out covered in grave clothes, and Jesus commands them to take off the grave clothes and let him go. Faith, compassion, and authoritative command are all involved in the carrying out of this miracle.

The purpose of the sign was to glorify God (verses 4 and

44), and also that the people there might believe that Jesus was sent by God. The actual consequences are that the miracle polarises opinion. On the one hand, many Jews believed in Jesus, and they were the ones who instigated the Palm Sunday acclamation as Jesus entered Jerusalem (John 12:16-18). Others, however, unbelievably, went and told the Pharisees, thereby setting in motion the final train of events that led to Jesus' crucifixion. In the meantime (11:54), Jesus had to take refuge in Ephraim, a town on the edge of the wilderness. We once again see how a sign sorts out those who are 'blind' from those who 'see'.

What became of Lazarus in the long run? In John 12:10 we learn that the chief priests thought of killing Lazarus as well; but they might not have succeeded. An early Christian writer called Epiphanius relates a tradition that Lazarus was thirty years old when he died, and once risen lived another thirty years.

Other healing encounters

The four stories that follow are examples of 'inner healing' – a term first used by the American healer Agnes Sanford in 1949. They differ from the stories we have visited thus far in being not overtly miraculous, because they do not involve suspension of natural laws. Neither do they involve demonisation. Nevertheless the people involved do need healing: healing of their personalities. It is often not bodies that need healing, but hearts and minds and relationships. This healing may not necessarily be healing from identifiable mental disorders such as clinical depression or schizophrenia. It may simply mean healing from things like inferiority complex, grief, long-standing bitterness, addictions, eating disorders, loneliness or estrangement, and many others which are definitely sicknesses of the soul and need dealing with if the sufferer is to be set free to live a normal Christian life. These disabilities cannot be seen, but are just as debilitating in their way as blindness or lameness.

28 Zacchaeus
(Luke 19:1-10)

The Zacchaeus story is actually a story about a man's salvation, and when the New Testament talks about 'salvation' (*soteria*) it means first and foremost setting free from sin. But as we saw in the Introduction, and in the Byway Words and Things, it overlaps with healing. Zacchaeus was a man in need of both.

Zacchaeus's story, which is very much a Luke-type story and is told only by him, is memorable and has a certain charm about it. The government farmed out tax-collecting, and those who collected the taxes were notorious for ripping off the tax-payers, and were hated for it. Zacchaeus is not merely a collector but a chief tax collector.

Yet he does seem to have been reaching out towards a better life, otherwise he would not have gone to the length of climbing a sycamore tree to see Jesus when his short stature meant he couldn't see over the heads of the Jericho crowds.

Jesus says, 'Zacchaeus, come down immediately. I must stay at your house today.' He might have known who it was because Zacchaeus was notorious, but then again it might have been his prophetic insight which had revealed it to him. It is interesting that he says he *must* stay at Zacchaeus's place. Why must he? It may mean that God had revealed to him that his orders were that there was a person called Zacchaeus whom he must visit. Or it may mean that he must go to be with him because the thing he must do is to seek out sinners.

Claude Montefiore was that highly unusual thing, a Jewish New Testament scholar. He obviously found much in the New Testament that was Jewish, but there was also something there that had no parallel in Judaism, and that was a reaching out to save the sinner: *going after him,* like the good shepherd or the woman seeking a lost coin (Luke 15:1-10).

The bystanders, however, had very different values. For them Zacchaeus was a waste of space, someone who was not worth saving and who would not be able to change anyway, so they were shocked by Jesus' action in going to Zacchaeus's house for tea. This challenges our attitudes and behaviour. No human being is a waste of space or 'scum', and no one is beyond the reach of God's love or of his power to change a life. It also reminds us that people often need to experience our love and friendship *before* they will seek salvation or healing, and therefore cutting ourselves off from social contact with them will not normally be the right thing to do.

The effect upon Zacchaeus was life-transforming. He engaged in radical repentance, for repentance is not only what you *feel* about your wrongdoing, but what you *do* about it. How serious his repentance was is indicated by his fourfold restitution. The Law required that you added only a fifth more on to what you were paying back (Leviticus 5:17; Numbers 5:7): one hundred and twenty per cent, not four hundred per cent! Yet Zacchaeus didn't *earn* salvation by doing that. He had already experienced loving acceptance by Jesus. That came first, before Zacchaeus did anything. The tax-collector's changed life was a response to that love.

Now here is where I think that healing came in. Jesus used of Zacchaeus a similar phrase to one he used of the bent woman. You will recall that he called her 'a daughter of Abraham'. Here Zacchaeus is called 'a son of Abraham'. The words are carefully chosen to remind each of these people that they belong. There has been a healing of relationships. Zacchaeus's small stature might have caused him problems. Perhaps it resulted in a feeling of inferiority. Perhaps it attracted bullying or created a sense of being an outsider. If that was the case, then Zacchaeus might not have taken up tax–collecting because of avarice, but as a result of not being able to gain acceptance and respect in the normal way, and deciding he might as well be hung for a sheep as for a lamb. So perhaps it was not the case that he became an outsider because he was a tax-collector, but that he became a tax-collector because he was already an outsider. Jesus put that right.

Zacchaeus was enabled to start afresh, and with a feeling of belonging.

29 **The Woman at the Well**
(John 4:4-30)

Pilgrims to the Holy Land, political situation permitting, are shown the site of this encounter, which now has an urban setting on the edge of the modern industrial city of Nablus. Mount Gerizim towers over the spot, and one can clearly see on it the temple where Samaritans, who still exist as a small sect to this day, worship God. The Old Testament nowhere refers to Jacob's Well, but it does speak of a plot of ground which that old patriarch gave to his son Joseph (Genesis 33:19). As the plot of ground would have been useless without a water supply, we can infer that a well was included in the gift. The name Nablus stems from that of a Roman town, Flavia Neapolis, built nearby in 67 CE. John doesn't mention this place, which therefore suggests that the story goes back to the time before Flavia Neapolis was built, and this counts towards its authenticity. It is not impossible that the source of the story was the chief character herself.

Jesus arrives from Jerusalem, having possibly left in something of a hurry to get away from the controversy he has caused there. The wording suggests that there was something imperative about his going through Samaria, a route he would not normally take, so his presence there might have been due to the Spirit's guidance. Jesus was a real man, much more than a real man, it is true, but a real man nevertheless, and he could become tired, thirsty and hungry like any other man.

He sends his disciples into the little town of Sychar to buy food, while he rests by the well in the noonday heat. A woman appears with a water jar, which is strange, because it is not the best time of the day to be coming for water. This perhaps indicates that she is shunned by the other women of the town because of her lifestyle.

Jesus asks her for a drink. He has no water pot with him so

cannot draw water for himself, but the woman is stunned. We can see no wrong in this, but Jesus has broken two, if not three, taboos:

1) *She is a woman*, and it was not the done thing for a rabbi to converse in the street with a woman. 2) *She is a Samaritan*. The Samaritans were descended from people who were settled in the middle part of the Holy Land by the King of Assyria after he had conquered it. They intermarried with the Jews who had remained in that area, and the religion they had was a watered-down version of the Jewish faith, which accepted the five books of the Law but not the prophets, looked to Mount Gerizim as the place to worship, not the Jerusalem Temple, and did believe in a Messiah-figure, but saw him simply as a prophet and teacher. In later years, they added on other cults and religions, causing a confusion of which this woman's lifestyle might have been a result. Jews had as little to do with them as possible. 3) *Her lifestyle* would have made it even less appropriate for Jesus to have spoken with her.

When she queries his request, Jesus makes some enigmatic remarks about 'living water', which excite her curiosity, and incidentally suggest to Christians a possible 'technique' for talking to non-Christians about the things of God. Enigmatic though Jesus' words are, they are deeply rooted in the Old Testament, where water is used as a word-picture for the Holy Spirit. One who has the Holy Spirit within him is fully alive, and to have received the Spirit is like having access to a stream of 'living water'. It isn't stagnant. It's always flowing (living), and there is always more of it than we have yet received. Anyone well acquainted with the Bible will be reminded of the vision that the prophet Ezekiel had of a river pouring out of the Temple (47:1-12), and also of the beautiful opening to Psalm 42:

> *'As the deer pants for streams of water,*
> *so my soul pants for you, O God.*
> *My soul thirsts for God, for the living God.*
> *When can I go and meet with God?'*

Jesus tells the woman that whoever drinks this water will never thirst again. He means that we go looking in all kinds of 'wells' for 'water' that will turn our existence into real living, but that none is sufficient to satisfy our souls: only the experience of God can do that.

To all this the woman replies, 'Sir, give me this water so that I won't get thirsty and have to keep coming here to draw water.' It could have been a harassed housewife's sarcastic reply, but it is more likely that she now realises that there is much, much more to this conversation than she at first thought, and much more to life than she has experienced, for her life thus far could scarcely have been truly happy or fulfilling. So when she asks for the living water it is the beginning of faith.

Jesus now apparently goes off at a tangent. He asks her to go and fetch her husband. This may be nothing but a means of leading into the word of prophecy he is about to give her; but it could also be a way of saying, 'If you are to receive this life-giving experience, your partner needs to be in on it too.' Sometimes marriages go wrong even among devout Christians when a couple see themselves as two distinct individuals, each with a separate calling, and fail to see themselves as a Spirit-filled partnership whose callings are bound up with one another. When she responds that she has no husband, Jesus, with prophetic insight, reminds her that she has had *five*, in fact, and that her present partner is not her husband. She is 'living in sin'.

One can only speculate about the woman's life story. That all her husbands had died is way beyond the bounds of probability, and we must be looking at a situation of multiple divorce. One divorce may be just misfortune; five is beginning to suggest difficult behaviour on her part and a chaotic lifestyle. The woman is a damaged individual. Perhaps she has failed to find satisfaction in any of her relationships and now needs to find rest for her soul in a relationship with God. Her reply seems to us like a red-herring, and perhaps it is. She wants what Jesus is offering, but he has trodden on a raw nerve, and people do tend to change the subject when a conversation seems likely to move into dangerous territory. It is more likely, however, that she means something relevant to the subject, that she takes the point that she must find forgiveness and turn over a new leaf. Should she therefore go to the Temple and offer sacrifice, but to which temple? Jesus then tells her that while religious differences are not unimportant, what is far more important is that those who worship God worship him in 'spirit and truth'. By this he means they should worship under the influence of the Holy Spirit, and in *reality*: being *honest* about themselves and their needs and the needs of the world, meaning what they say, and being able to be honest and real because they know that they are loved by God. They have encountered his love, which is unconditional, and when they have experienced a love like that, they are free to be honest and real. Without that love, they would tend to retreat from honesty and reality into denial, because the truth about themselves would be too much to cope with.

The woman has found faith enough to find salvation, yet she is still confused by all the sects and cults of her homeland, and the differences between Jew and Samaritan. Perhaps, she says, when Messiah comes, he will sort it all out. Then Jesus says, with an openness that would be dangerous in Jerusalem but doesn't matter here, 'I am he.'

We look nowadays, too, in all kinds of places for the things that will satisfy our souls' longing for a depth and quality of life way beyond mere existence, and sometimes our quest takes us into a chaos of short-term relationships or conflicting religious ideas. Meanwhile, right under our noses, is the one who has the water of life, Jesus the Messiah.

As a postscript, note the grace and beauty of Jesus' character. Being exhausted and thirsty in the heat of the day is not the best condition in which to be faced with someone's need for counselling or an evangelistic opportunity; but Jesus does not avoid the encounter or try to make an appointment for a more convenient time. He is there for her, when she needs him to be. A ministry that heals can be costly.

30 The Reinstatement of Simon Peter
(John 21:1-19)

The passage begins with an account of a miraculous catch of fish. Now there is a similar story in Luke's gospel (Luke 5:1-11), but that story has a very different context, for whereas this incident occurs right at the end of Jesus' earthly ministry, the Lucan story stands right at the beginning, and forms part of the call of the first disciples. Matthew's and Mark's stories of the call of the first disciples are strikingly abrupt. Jesus walks along the seashore, sees Simon, Andrew, James and John mending their nets, says, 'Follow me', and up they get and follow him. Luke tells a different story. Jesus, he says, requisitioned Simon Peter's boat so that he could stand in the prow as if it were a pulpit and address the people standing on the beach. Then, when it was time to go, Jesus, who was nobody's debtor, told Simon to launch out into the deep and let down his nets for a catch. Simon protested that they had been working all night and had taken nothing, implying that his fisherman's experience told him he was unlikely to catch anything just then. But, being an amiable man, he agreed to do what the master had said. Whereupon the boat was swamped with fish and nearly sank! Peter's reply on that occasion could not have been invented, and the story was surely in any case handed down by him. 'Go away from me, Lord,' he said, 'for I am a sinful man.' Jesus' reply was, 'Fear not; from now on you will be catching men.'

The similarity between the two stories has led many commentators to assume that they are variant accounts of the same incident. What I want to suggest, however, is that they describe two distinct incidents, one occurring at the beginning of Jesus' earthly ministry, and the other occurring after he had risen from the dead, at the beginning of his heavenly ministry; and that they occurred that way for the benefit of the one who was to be the leader of the disciples, Simon Peter.

We learn a lot about Peter in the gospels. He emerges as a strong, capable fisherman, a family man, generous-hearted and with considerable leadership gifts. He also appears to have faults, and while I hesitate to dwell on his faults, Peter being one of the greatest of all Christians, it does appear as if he allowed stories to be told against himself for our learning. On that basis and no other, I feel able to mention what those faults might have been.

Firstly, he would open his mouth without thinking. On the Mount of Transfiguration in the middle of an awesome experience of God's presence, he had suggested making three little booths on the mountain (Mark 9:5). Again, Peter was an impulsive person who would commit himself only too readily to a course of action but then be unable to follow it through. Matthew tells how once, when Jesus came to the disciples' storm-tossed boat walking on the water, Peter suggested that he, too, might walk on the water. To begin with, he found he could do so, but then he lost his nerve and began to sink (Matt.14:22-33). His glibness and impulsiveness had come together on the night when Jesus was arrested. At that time Peter had sworn to Jesus that he was prepared to lay down his life for him (John 13:37). According to Matthew, what he said on that occasion was, 'Even if all fall away on account of you, I never will' (26:33). Jesus' reply must have utterly dismayed him. He informed Peter that before the cock crowed Peter would deny three times that he knew him. That was how it turned out. Peter had been bold enough to follow the posse that arrested Jesus into the courtyard of the high priest's palace, but it was there, where a charcoal fire (an *anthrakia*) was burning, that he three times responded to probing questions from bystanders to the effect that he did not know Jesus, the last time with great vehemence. Then the 'cock crew' (probably not a literal cock but a Roman bugle) and Peter, in a devastating moment of shame and self-knowledge, went outside and wept bitterly.

Later, after their Master had risen from the dead, we find most of the disciples back in Galilee. Peter suddenly said, 'I'm going fishing', and where Peter led, others followed; so off they went. Why did Peter want to go fishing? The previous weeks since Jesus' crucifixion had not been an emotional roller-coaster; they had been an emotional *mountain range*; and Peter in particular would still have been haunted by what he had done. He would have been desperately in need of inner healing, for without it whenever he sought to fulfil his calling and give leadership to the new Christian community, there would always have been a little voice inside his head (*not* God's voice) accusing him of being unsuitable for the job, of being unworthy of it, and of how it was seriously inappropriate that someone who had let his Lord down so badly should be in his position. Therefore there would be a need to learn lessons; there would be a need for restoration, a need to know that a line had been drawn under the whole sorry episode and that he could move forward: closure, in fact. In any case it had all been too much. Peter was no doubt emotionally exhausted; they all were; and when men are like that, what they need is a piece of normality. The lake, the comradeship, the fishing: that was all they needed right then. They might or might not have been right in seeking the old life for a while, but Jesus was to meet them where they were, whether or not that was where they should have been.

I believe that what followed was a deliberate re-run of Peter's original call. Once again, Jesus appears on the shore. This time he directs them to cast their nets on the other side of the ship, and once again there is a huge catch of fish. But now, when Peter realises that the stranger on the shore is, in fact, the Lord, he does not say, 'Go away from me, Lord' (Luke 5:8). Instead, he throws his coat round himself and slops through the water to be with him. On the first occasion he had wanted Jesus to go away. This time he wants to be with him.

On the shore he finds an *anthrakia*, a charcoal fire like the one in the high priest's courtyard. The smell would bring back memories for Peter, as odours tend to do. After their shared breakfast, Jesus engages Peter in a conversation which is probing and painful, but which results in Peter's healing. Commentators might question my interpretation of the story thus far, but would be virtually unanimous in seeing the conversation as Jesus' way of restoring Peter.

If we are to understand properly what was going on in that conversation, we need to pay careful attention to the language. Jesus begins by addressing Peter as, 'Simon, son of John.' That is his real name, but what has happened to, 'Peter, man of rock', the noble name that Jesus once gave him? It's as if he can't wear it right now. Then Jesus asks him if he loves him 'more than these', and those words are a literal translation of the Greek, which is as ambiguous in the original as it is in translation. Jesus could be asking if Peter loves him more than the appurtenances of his fishing way of life; but I believe he is overwhelmingly more likely, given the context, to be referring to Peter's boast that others might leave him, but Peter would not. This was a painful but necessary reminder of what Peter had said.

And then, the way that Jesus words his questions and answers to Peter varies significantly. It is not the case that each time Jesus simply says, 'Do you love me?' and that each time Peter replies, 'Yes, Lord, I love you', and then Jesus responds, 'Feed my sheep.' The Greek words used are such that they could be translated thus:

> Simon, son of John, do you **love** me?
> Yes, Lord, you know that *I'm* **fond** *of* you.
> *Feed* my *lambs*.
> Simon, son of John, do you **love** me?
> Yes, Lord, you know that *I'm* **fond** *of* you.
> *Tend* my *sheep*.
> Simon, son of John, are you **fond** *of* me?
> (rattled) Lord, you know everything.
> You know that *I'm* **fond** *of* you.
> *Feed my sheep.*

In his first and second questions Jesus uses *agapao*. When he addresses the question for the third time, Jesus uses *phileo*; and in all three responses Peter uses *phileo*.

Jesus wants Peter to say what he means and mean what he says, and as he learns to do this he will become steadily more mature. At first he will feed lambs, then he will help to tend the sheep, and then he will feed the sheep, in fact (according to the Greek), lead them out to find pasture. Peter has learnt his lesson. He is not going to brag any more or be glib. Jesus follows up with an enigmatic reminder of the death Peter is to die. Tradition indeed has it that he was crucified like his Lord. It is as if Jesus is saying, 'One day, Peter, you will die a violent death for following me. Are you still prepared to follow me, knowing that?' Peter says nothing. He has given up making extravagant claims for himself. And then Jesus – as he had commissioned Peter those three years previously in the Galilean springtime when there was the first miraculous catch of fish – recommissions him. 'Follow me,' he says once again.

The story is deeply moving and remarkable for its psychological insight. It could scarcely have been fabricated, and because it must have occurred after the Resurrection constitutes evidence for Jesus' rising from the dead. For those times and places where Christians are being persecuted, it is a reassurance that people who buckle under persecution can perhaps start again. For our own time, it is an encouragement that when people are conscious of wrong within they can, through Jesus, be healed, draw a line under a guilty past, and begin again.

section 3
A tour of the healing stories in Acts

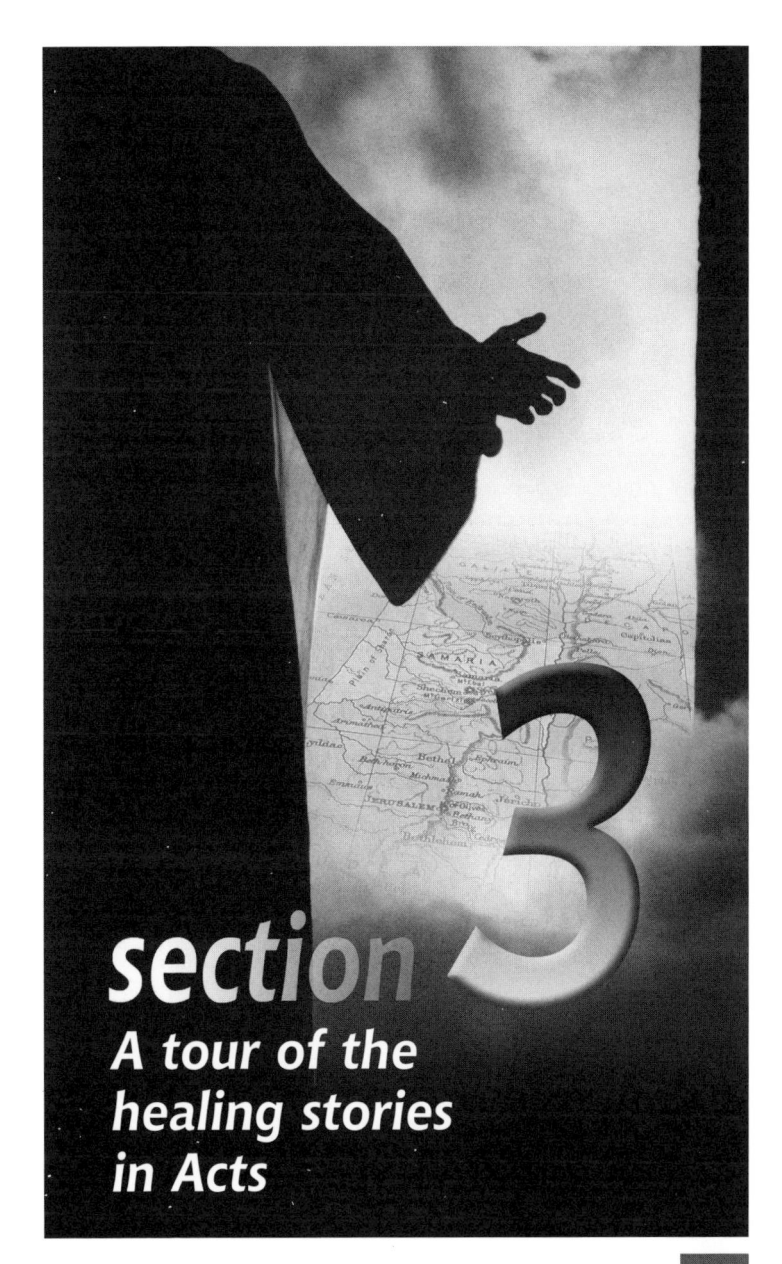

Preliminary briefing

We now land in the middle of the second book of Luke's two-volume work, and our visits to the various stories become chronological and geographical, and rather less complicated, because there is only one source that we can look at. (For more information about the author, see Byway Doctor Luke.)

I hope that the following selection of passages will whet your appetite to read the whole of the book of Acts. Professor James Dunn was surely right when he identified Acts as the most exciting book in the Bible. The narrative, always vivid, usually swift moving, sometimes violent, strides on its way from Jerusalem through Samaria and Antioch, and on through Asia Minor (Turkey) and Greece, ending up in Rome in a somewhat open-ended way, as if the Gospel is still carrying on to the ends of the Earth, even after Luke has stopped writing about it. The book reads like a novel, but when you've read a novel, you can put it down and it need not affect your lifestyle one bit, however exciting the story was.

Acts is not a novel. It claims to be telling the truth, and it can often be demonstrated that it is. Moreover, the truth affects the reader, who has to make a decision and then take a stance about what has been read. Detachment is not an option. For us Christians, this story of frail, flawed men and women nevertheless going to the ends of the Earth, facing incredible hardships miles out of their comfort-zones, and being followed often by miracles, sometimes by mayhem, but always by people finding healing, salvation and a new life, challenges us to ask whether the Church today should be like this, and if it should, why isn't it?

Passages to be visited

31 The Lame Man at the Temple Gate – 3:1-10, 16; 4:8-17
32 Wonders in Jerusalem – 5:12-16
33 Spirit and Sorcery in Samaria – 8:6-25
34 Saul's Recovery of Sight – 9:17-19

35 Aeneas healed of Paralysis – 9:32-35
36 Dorcas raised from the Dead – 9:36-41
37 A Power-encounter with Elymas the Sorcerer – 13:4-12
38 The Crippled Man healed at Lystra – 14:8-20
39 The Slave Girl at Philippi – 16:16-18
40 Paul's Ephesus Mission – 19:1-20
41 Eutychus's Death and Resuscitation – 20:9-12
42 Healings on Malta – 28:1-9

31 The Lame Man at the Temple Gate
(3:1-10, 16; 4:8-17)

A great deal of water (living water?) has flowed under the bridge in the short space of time since we left Peter with the risen Jesus by the lakeside. Jesus has returned to his Father (Acts 1), and some ten days later, while the disciples were gathered in an upper room, they had a remarkable, powerfully spiritual experience which they knew to be God's 'pouring out' of the Holy Spirit upon them (Acts 2). They were no longer fearful and hiding away from the Jewish authorities, but went about openly proclaiming that Jesus is the Christ. That meant going regularly to the temple, where, one day, Peter and John found a lame man being brought to beg at the Gate Beautiful.

The lame man begged the apostles not for healing but for money. Peter, as usual the spokesman, said, 'Look at us!' and we do not know why he should have said that, because it has no parallel in Jesus' healing methods. Perhaps if you had asked Peter why he did it he could not have told you either. It was simply what the Holy Spirit guided him to do so, on that occasion. Certainly it arrested the man's attention. Beggars do not normally look people in the eye, and it might have kindled faith in him to receive the authoritative command Peter gave him. 'Silver or gold I do not have,' said Peter, 'but what I have I give you. In the name of Jesus Christ of Nazareth, walk.' Helped to his feet by the apostles, the beggar began to walk, and leap, and praise God, overjoyed by his healing. It is a fulfilment of Isaiah 35:6: 'Then shall the lame man leap as a hart.' The onlookers' response was amazement.

It is a cue for a preaching opportunity. Where there is public healing in Acts, preaching of the Gospel is never far away. We get the impression that the ministry of healing should not be separated from the message. In his preaching, Peter offers an explanation of what has happened:

'By faith in the name of Jesus, this man whom you see and know was made strong. It is Jesus' name and the faith that comes through him that has given this complete healing to him, as you can all see' (3:16).

Faith was apparently involved in the healing. Perhaps it was the man's faith – a flash of recognition that before him stood a man of God who was going to change his life, and that was the grain of mustard seed that was enough to connect him with the power of the name of Jesus. If it was not the man's own faith, then presumably it was on the strength of the apostles' faith that he was healed. Note that Peter says the faith comes *through Jesus*. Faith is itself a gift of God. We cannot puff ourselves up into a state of faith by human will-power; it is a gift which is given us, and this is true whether we are speaking of an attitude of faith in general, or faith that a particular thing is happening at a particular time. This does not mean that you have either been given it or you haven't, and there is nothing you can do about it. For God can be asked to create faith in you or increase the faith you already have, and he will do so, by whatever means is right for you.

But it is faith in the *name* of Jesus that is involved. Acts has sometimes been misleadingly called 'the Gospel of the Holy Spirit'. The Holy Spirit does the works in Acts, it is true, but this happens when Jesus is revered and worshipped and kept at the centre of things. What, however, is meant by the expression 'the name of Jesus', which occurs not only here but several times in Peter's and John's defence of their behaviour before the Sanhedrin in chapter 4:8-17?

When we use the word 'name', we mean no more than a label by which to identify someone. In Bible times it meant much more:

• If you operated in someone's name you carried his or her authority. We still sometimes use it this way, as in the expression, 'Halt in the name of the law!' The apostles carried the authority of Jesus, and there are many situations where a faithful Christian today will carry his authority. It is worth remembering, though, that we *carry* this authority only if we are *under* authority. The uniformed policeman on duty has authority to hold up the traffic, but he has this authority only as long as he remains *under* authority. Once he has ceased to be a policeman, attempting to hold up the traffic would not be a good idea!

• Name meant reputation, and here, too, there are modern parallels. We say of some local lad made good that he has 'made quite a name for himself'. When we praise the name of Jesus, we are praising all he has shown himself to be, and wanting him to be more widely known.

So far so good. Up to now we have been able to understand the concept of 'name' by analogy with our own experience, but there were other ways it was used in Bible times which are strange to us.

• It meant the very personality of the named person. Jacob means 'supplanter', and the name suited him because that was what he was, a scheming rogue. Later, however, after many adventures and learning the hard way where his schemes could lead him, Jacob found himself wrestling with God in a lonely spot. He attempted to wrestle God's name out of him but God would not tell him, because another thing about names was that it was believed that if you knew a person's name you had power over him. God, however, gave Jacob a new name, Israel, because he had wrestled with God and had prevailed (Genesis 32:22-32). Often in the Bible people are given new names when they take on new natures. Simon becomes Peter, 'Rock' (John 1:42), and Joseph of

105

Cyprus becomes Barnabas, 'Son of Consolation', because he was such a great encourager.

• Stranger still, the name of God could mean the power and presence of God. The Temple was built for God's Name to dwell there (1 Kings 5:5), and the angel who guarded the wandering Israelites had God's Name in him (Exodus 23:21).

All these meanings of 'name' are involved in the ministry of healing. The healing person operates with Christ's identity, on Christ's authority, with a concern for his glory, in a Christ-like way, and with his power and presence. The healer may be penniless, unschooled and ordinary (see Acts 4:13), but operating in the name of Jesus he or she will be effective. Lacking any other power, he knows he needs the power of God. Conversely, ability and riches may even work against effectiveness in this ministry. F. F. Bruce, commenting on this story, tells how Thomas Aquinas called upon Pope Innocent II once when the latter was counting a large sum of money. 'You see, Thomas', said the Pope, 'the Church can no longer say, "Silver and gold have I none".' 'True, Holy Father,' said Thomas, 'and neither can she now say, "Arise and walk".'

Words and Things

All the Greek words used for health and healing occur in the New Testament in Acts chapters 3 and 4.

3:7 'Immediately his feet and ankles were *made strong*' (*steroo*)

3:16 'His name has made this man *strong*' (*steroo*) 'Faith . . . has given this man perfect *health*' (*holokeria*) or '*wholeness*' (only place 'wholeness' is found in the New Testament!)

4:9 'By what means this man has been *healed*' (*sozo*)

4:10 'By him this man is standing before you *well*' (*hugies*)

> 4:14 'The man that had been *healed*' *(therapeuo)*
> 4:22 'This *sign of healing*' *(iasis)*
> 4:30 'You stretch out your hand to *heal*' *(iaomai)*
>
> *Therapeuo* and *iaomai* are the most frequently used words for healing in the New Testament. They mean virtually the same thing. *Sozo* might be a little different, because it and its derivative *soteria* often mean 'saving from sin', and this raises the question of whether 'salvation' and 'healing' amount to the same thing, or *sozo* is used because it *just happens* to mean both 'heal' and 'save from sin', or if the two are used because salvation and healing overlap. Certainly, salvation often brings healing with it in one form or another.
>
> The way all these words tumble out suggests there is a comprehensiveness about what Jesus does through his apostles. You name it; he does it!

32 Wonders in Jerusalem
(5:12-16)

The twelfth verse, with its statement that '*the apostles* performed many miraculous signs and wonders among the people', might just give the impression that apostles do healings, and ordinary rank-and-file Christians do not, and since there are no longer such people as apostles (if you discount Anglican and Catholic bishops, who are regarded as their successors), there is no longer any gift of healing. On that question, refer to the Introduction.

At the time of the infancy of the Church, the healing ministry might have been largely confined to the apostles until such time as wise, mature leadership developed in the Christian community. Certainly, verses 13 and 14 suggest that people were reluctant to join the Christians because, presumably, of what it might cost them, but the Christians were nevertheless respected. It was a kind of missionary situation with many parallels down the centuries of Christian history.

Verse 15 is a little controversial too. When the people laid their sick on mats in the sunshine in the hope that Peter's shadow might heal them, were they indeed healed as a result, or was that just superstition? If it was the latter, then although Peter and the apostles did come and heal them as in verse 16, it had nothing to do with Peter's shadow. A group of old manuscripts of the New Testament called 'the Western Text' adds to verse 15, 'for they were all set free from every sickness which each of them had.' So as far as the copyists who made that alteration were concerned, yes, we were intended to understand that the people were healed by Peter's shadow. The question is an important one, because in the Roman Catholic tradition much healing is believed to take place through contact with sacred objects or plunging into sacred springs. The question is, is this to be expected as one of the ways God works, or is it superstition? The Byway Objects, Substances, Shrines and Sacrament might help to clear up this vexed question.

33 Spirit and Sorcery in Samaria
(8:6-25)

Much has happened since the time of the last passage we visited. The disciples have begun to suffer persecution. Stephen, the first Christian to die for his faith, has been stoned to death. Life having become very difficult in Jerusalem, Christians begin to move out, but they take the good news about Jesus with them. God is bringing good out of evil, as he often does. Philip, an impressive Spirit-driven character, normally known as Philip the Evangelist and not to be confused with the disciple Philip, goes and evangelises a town in Samaria. It is tempting to believe that it might have been Sychar, for John the Baptist had worked near there, and it was there that Jesus had met the woman at the well; but we are not told the name of the place, and it might have been virgin territory as far as Christian preaching was concerned. Philip's main purpose was to tell the people about Jesus, but his mission was accompanied by miraculous healings, and it was because of those miracles that people paid close attention to what he said. A theme is beginning to appear here, for throughout Acts the preaching of Jesus is accompanied by 'signs and wonders', and these not only draw an audience but help to confirm the truth of what is said. There is a contrast here with the miracles of Jesus described in the first three gospels, for there Jesus seemed to wish to keep his healings a secret. In Acts, God 'confirms his word with signs following'.

But there is something missing from Philip's converts. They are baptised, but they have not received the Holy Spirit. John Gunstone, a British Anglican priest, says he used to tell people who were to be confirmed in his church that when the bishop laid his hands upon them they would receive the Holy Spirit, but they were not to expect that they would *feel* anything. He later came to believe that he was in error in that respect. For here in this passage it is clear that Philip realises, and perhaps the converts themselves realise, that nothing has happened to them; they neither look nor feel any different, so they know they have not yet received the Spirit. The implication is obvious. If you receive the Holy Spirit you will *be aware of it* in some way. Converts today speak of a deep peace or joy, an intense desire to share what has happened to them and celebrate it, a sense of having been loved and accepted, a glorious feeling of 'yes!' and usually major changes in their moral character and values.

The absence of the Spirit is solved by their having Peter and John come down from Jerusalem and lay hands on them, and then they receive the Holy Spirit, and of course they must have known it. What Peter and John did that Philip couldn't do, though, we do not know.

One of the converts turns out to be a sinister character: Simon Magus, or Simon the Sorcerer. Simon has a huge reputation in Samaria with its sects, cults and superstition, but when he sees the power that Philip exercises, his offbeat reaction is to get himself baptised, in the hope, presumably, that this will be the first step to getting some of that power for himself. And when Peter and John come down from Jerusalem and he witnesses the effect of their ministry on the new converts, he offers the apostles money. (Ever since, payment for Christian ministry has been called 'Simony'.) Peter responds with a blistering rebuke. 'To hell with you and your money,' he says (a good translation of the Greek!), and he urges Simon to repent because he is a prisoner of sin and his heart is not right with God. However, Simon's response is not so much to repent, as to pray that none of the evil Peter threatened him with will, in fact, happen. He is perhaps 'too far gone' to understand what repentance is.

At this point, Simon Magus disappears from the pages of Acts, and Luke never mentions him again; but he certainly does not depart from the pages of history, and grows into a huge challenge for Christianity. He is said to have continued to build up a following for himself in Samaria, and then moved on to Rome in the reign of the Emperor Claudius and built up an even bigger following there, being honoured by a statue dedicated to 'Simon the Holy God'. He is also said to have gone about with a woman called Helena, a former slave girl whom he declared to be 'thought and conception of the divine mind' made flesh (all angelic power and all material universe having proceeded from the divine mind.) Finally, he is reputed to have had himself buried alive in Rome, promising that on the third day he would rise again: but it did not happen!

The problem that Simon posed to the Christian was not so much that he opposed Christianity, but rather that he corrupted it from within. He taught a whole system of thought called Gnosticism, which bore a superficial resemblance to Christianity and must have confused the ill-informed. Gnosticism taught that spirit was good, and matter was evil.

Its equivalent to conversion was to have 'knowledge' disclosed to one. Hence the name *gnosis*, which means 'knowledge'.

The point of the Acts story is that Christianity has nothing to do with magic, and the message for us is that healing by the occult or magic is to be avoided. This alternative form of 'healing' has continued to be a challenge to Christianity because it is often not understood how it differs from Christian healing. The dangers are set out in this passage from a pamphlet by Leonard Wilson, former warden of the Anglican Healing Centre at Crowhurst, England:

'The first result of occult healing is loss of pain, and what can be called a sign or wonder has happened physically. There follows an alienation of personality. . . . Something within a person becomes cut off. They might be physically fit, but they have lost something of vitality. If you are discerning, you can see it in their eyes. The sparkle has gone, unless a fear or hate gives it a false energy. There is inevitably a darkness and a coldness towards God. One frequently hears such people say, "I have lost my sense of God's nearness."

'. . . They are always affected in their human relationships. There is always somebody who becomes their enemy, or the source of their dislike. Talking to people who have been involved in this, they describe a character who has hurt them or treated them badly. . . . Then you meet them and you cannot believe it is the person you have been hearing about.'

This is, of course, the view of one man, albeit highly experienced, but it does correspond with some of my pastoral experiences. The impression I get is that occult healing can tap into spiritual forces which will indeed cure physical symptoms or even the conditions that cause them, but are like a very toxic and unproven drug, clearing up conditions in the body at the cost of poisoning the soul. That is too high a price to pay.

Magic and Miracle

For many people, the miracle stories of the New Testament savour of 'magic', and if we could not distinguish them from magic we would have to draw one or other of two conclusions:

- Magic is a superstitious practice which humanity has outgrown, and should therefore be rejected; and, by the same token, belief in miracles should be rejected as well.
- Magic is not to be rejected, so we therefore pick up belief in miracles along with a lot of superstitious ideas, and cannot tell the difference between the two.

For the New Testament writers there is clearly an enormous difference between the two; in fact they are opposed to each other, as we can see in the story of Simon Magus and the stories of Elymas and Paul's mission in Ephesus (Acts 13:4-12). This opposition harks back to the Old Testament, where the most important text is Deuteronomy 18:10-13:

'Let no-one be found among you who sacrifices his son or daughter in the fire, who practises divination or sorcery, interprets omens, engages in witchcraft, or casts spells, or who is a medium or spiritist or who consults the dead. Anyone who does these things is detestable to the Lord, and because of these detestable practices the Lord your God will drive out those nations before you. You must be blameless before the Lord your God.'

Leviticus 19:31 condemns spiritism, and Isaiah 47:12-15 condemns astrology. The death penalty is prescribed for magic (Exodus 22:18; Leviticus 20:6, 27), but it is important that in Acts 19:18-20, in the different world of the New Testament, magicians are not burnt. They are converted and their books are burnt instead! Magic and magicians are now to be dealt with differently. Nevertheless, both Testaments see a huge difference between true religion and magic, which are in total opposition to each other.

It is worth noting that the philosophers of biblical times also tended to take a dim view of magic. Plato condemned it, and Pliny the Elder considered it detestable.

But what are the differences between magic and Christian healing?

• Magic is often done for a fee. Christian ministry is offered freely.

• Magicians assume that no single spiritual power has authority over the universe. The Creation Story told by the Babylonians tells how the god Marduk used magic in his fight against monsters created by Tiamat, another of the gods. By contrast, Christians believe that there is only one God, who is in total charge of the universe.

• The difference between magic and religion is that while magic recognises the existence of spiritual beings, it seeks to manipulate them for its own ends. Religion too recognises their existence, but instead of manipulating them it worships or reveres them. Christianity, of course, reveres and worships only one God, the Creator.

• When a Christian seeks the aid of God, he recognises that he may or may not get what he desires, depending on whether what he asks is good for him or not. The magician, on the other hand, uses spells, rituals, incantations, potions, gems, amulets, curse tablets, whatever, to achieve his ends, and believes that if he gets the ingredients or the formulae right, what he wants will happen *automatically.*

- The magician of New Testament times picked and chose from various religions anything that he thought might 'work', which was why the seven sons of Sceva tried to adjure demons by the name of Jesus. The Christian, on the other hand, believes that God has revealed himself in Jesus, and the guidance contained in that revelation is sufficient, and the Holy Spirit indwelling believers renders the use of all those other powers unnecessary.
- Magic is amoral. The magician believes that the powers upon which he draws are not interested in whether his intentions are good or evil. Christianity is, by contrast, an intensely moral faith. We are to be holy because God is holy, and what makes him holy is that he is good (Isaiah 5:16). Wrongdoing puts up a barrier between humanity and God (Isaiah 59:1, 2), and by the same token it is the good person, obedient to God (1 John 3:22) whose prayers have power with God, and around whom remarkable things happen. As James says, 'The prayer of a righteous man is powerful and effective' (James 5:16).

34 Saul's Recovery of Sight
(9:10-19)

Saul, later Paul, began by being ferociously anti-Christian. In fact he had been involved in the stoning to death of the first Christian martyr, Stephen (8:1). Then, on the road to Damascus to continue persecuting Christians, Saul had a remarkable experience of God, which was to turn his attitude round completely, and was led, temporarily blinded, into Damascus. In Damascus a Christian called Ananias lived close to God, sufficiently close to know God's voice when he heard it. God told him to go to the house of Judas in Straight Street, which still exists in that ancient city, and enquire at the house of one Judas for Saul.

Judas is a common name, but is there perhaps a bit of symbolism here? Saul was still living in 'the house of Judas', but all that was to change. God also told him that Saul had seen a vision of Ananias coming to place his hands on him. Ananias, aware of Saul's fearsome reputation, was not at all struck on the idea, but he did what he was told. Visions confirming visions or other guidance are not unknown in healing literature today. Ananias visited Saul, and when he prayed for him, something like scales fell from Saul's eyes and he was able to see again. (Apparently, this cannot be identified as a known eye condition.) The healing was accompanied by the laying on of hands, and that had a twofold function. It not only ministered healing to Saul; it was also accompanied by his being filled with the Spirit. We previously saw this gesture used by Peter and John on the new converts in Samaria (8:17), and it is still widely used in the churches today with the same significance.

What can be learnt from this story?

First, we can learn that healing, and laying on of hands, can be done by apparently ordinary people and is not confined to apostles, for whatever position Ananias might have held in the church, there is no evidence that he was an apostle. Second, it was against 'cessationism'; this passage tells us that healing was entrusted not just to apostles but to others in leadership in the Church.

Ananias is an obscure person. He plays a 'bit part' in the drama of Acts, then disappears off-stage, never to return. Yet his obedience to God made him a vital link in a chain. I wonder what would *not* have happened if his distaste for Saul had led him to say 'No' to God. Behind many a great, godly and well-known Christian there is often an obscure priest, teacher or friend who led him or her to Christ. Most people have heard of the great American evangelist Dr Billy Graham; comparatively few have heard of Mordecai Ham, the evangelist under whose preaching he was converted. Many Methodists revere the name of W. E. Sangster, whom Billy Graham himself called 'a preacher without peer in the whole world'. Few, however, know the name Francis Wimpory, the Sunday School teacher in a back-street mission in London, who first invited the young Sangster to take the step of becoming a Christian. Obscure, ordinary people, if they cultivate a close walk with God, which means learning to identify his voice and obey it, may be the means of converting or helping someone who later goes on to do great things for God.

35 Aeneas Healed of Paralysis
(9:32-35)

Similarities in wording are noticeable between this passage and the stories of how Jesus healed paralysed people in the gospels (Mark 2:1-12; John 5:1-15), especially the command to tidy up one's bed (or pick up one's stretcher) and walk. We will see other similarities in the story of Dorcas which follows. This is surely no accident, and is probably Luke's way of saying that the works Jesus did, the disciples were also doing.

Lydda is nowadays the site of Lod, Israel's main airport, and Sharon is the name of Israel's flat coastal plain. All over this populous, extensive area people saw Aeneas out and about, and turned to the Lord as a result. It is another example of the miraculous compelling people to make a decision.

36 Dorcas Raised from the Dead
(9:36-42)

Immediately after the healing of Aeneas, Peter is called to Joppa, a seaport on the coast about ten miles from Lydda. There a woman called 'Gazelle', which is what is meant by Tabitha in Aramaic and Dorcas in Greek, has just died, and since she was a lovely person, well known for her good works and for being good with her hands, her death has caused much grief; and Peter finds a room full of widows who have benefited from her help, weeping and showing the clothes she has made for them. Peter puts them all out; and already we are beginning to think the story is a little like Jesus' healing of Jairus's daughter (Mark 5:35-43). But the resemblance becomes even more striking when Peter takes her by the hand with the words *tabitha cumi,* because the command is only one letter different from Jesus' words to Jairus's little daughter: *talitha cumi.*

There can be no question of the two stories being variants of the same story because the locations and names are so different, and there are eye-witness features confirming their authenticity, but this only highlights how strange the resemblances are. And then we noticed in the story of Aeneas, too, that there were resemblances to Jesus' healings of paralysed men. If we were to scour Acts, we would come up with even more passages resembling stories and sayings in the gospels. For instance, where Jesus at his crucifixion says, 'Father, forgive them for they know not what they do', we find Stephen at his execution saying, 'Lord, lay not this sin to their charge.'

What is going on? Surely, however we explain the resemblances, they are a subtle way of saying that Jesus' disciples are now continuing his work. This confirms Jesus' words in John 14:12:

'I tell you the truth, anyone who has faith in me will do what I have been doing. He will do even greater things than these, because I am going to the Father.'

Once again, the consequence of the miracle is that people are led to God. Some words of the Scottish Christian writer Tom Smail are an apt comment on these miracles:

'Only when the Holy Spirit moves and the whole range of New Testament things start happening and the Church is gathered and shaped into the Community of His Body, does the Church begin to function relevantly and effectively, so that Christ and the claims we make for Him become real issues for people. The healing of a little girl may say to a whole watching street of neighbours that Jesus is Lord, in a way that all the words spoken in the Church, at which most of them are never present, can quite fail to do. The Lord Jesus has walked out of the religious in-world and come down our street: the Kingdom has again drawn near and shown itself to be among us, and it becomes in a new way an urgent question for us what we shall do with the King.'

Then Peter went off and lodged by the seashore with Simon the Tanner. Tanners were permanently 'unclean' because of their contact with dead animals, but this does not appear to have worried Peter. The Christian Gospel is for everybody, clean or unclean.

37 A Power Encounter with Elymas the Sorcerer
(13:4-12)

We catch up with Saul in Cyprus a few years later. He has now become a leading Christian missionary, having, along with Barnabas, been commissioned for this work by the Church in Antioch under the Spirit's guidance. Their missionary tour has taken them all through Cyprus and they have ended up at Paphos, the seat of government, situated at the western end of the island. There they have an audience with Sergius Paulus, whom Luke, an accurate historian, correctly describes as Proconsul. (Roman provinces were of two kinds: Imperial and Senatorial. Armies were stationed in the former, not the latter. Imperial provinces were ruled over by Procurators and Senatorial by Proconsuls. Cyprus was Senatorial. So Luke gets his title right.) Sergius was in all probability the same person as a Sergius Paulus who was Curator of the Tiber in the reign of the Emperor Claudius.

The Proconsul has with him a character called Bar-Jesus or Elymas. Bar-Jesus means 'Son of Jesus', which is not as surprising as it seems because Jesus was a common name, but it nevertheless sounds deeply ironic when you consider that the man, a renegade Jew and an astrologer, was trying to divert Sergius Paulus from the Christian faith.

What follows is the sort of thing called in some modern healing literature a 'power encounter', which is to say an incident in which the spiritual power of Christianity is shown to be superior to that of paganism or another faith. The encounter seems to have marked a turning point in Saul's spiritual growth, because Luke tells us here that Saul is also called Paul, and Paul he remains thereafter. It is as if, like Jacob or Peter, a new name is applied to him to represent a new nature. He is now 'filled with the Spirit', and the tense of the Greek verb means not that he was a man who happened to be already full of the Spirit, but that he was filled with the Spirit right then and there, to do what he had to do. Now Saul had already been filled with the Spirit when Ananias had laid hands on him at his conversion (Acts 9:17), but here it happens again. Filling with the Holy Spirit is clearly not a one-off event. A person can go on being filled with the Spirit again and again, and will need to be.

In the Spirit, Paul does something to Elymas that is the opposite of healing. He roundly denounces him:

'You are a child of the devil and an enemy of everything that is right! You are full of all kinds of deceit and trickery. Will you never stop perverting the right ways of the Lord?' (v10)

He then strikes Elymas with blindness, but his blindness, like Saul's own blindness when he was converted, is blindness for a reason. This is the mercy of God, because there is the hope that Elymas, too, might be converted and regain his sight. For his part, Sergius Paulus 'believes', which is Luke's usual term for being converted. In confirmation of this, F. F. Bruce says that Sir William Ramsay found evidence that the Proconsul's daughter, Sergia Paula, became a Christian, and likewise her son Gaius Caristonius Fronto, a member of a prominent Pisidian Antioch family.

This very-well-attested power encounter has its parallels in Church history. Ian Finlay in his book on Columba, who preached Christianity in Scotland in the seventh century CE, recounts the wonderful story of how Columba went to the city of Inverness to confront the Pictish King Brude. Finding the gates of the city closed against him, Columba chalked a cross on the gates, calling out in a loud voice the words of Psalm 46:1, 2: '*God is our refuge and strength, an ever-present help in trouble. Therefore we will not fear, though the earth give way and the mountains fall into the heart of the sea.*' Then he 'smote' the gates, which burst open. It was the beginning of the end of paganism in Scotland. One role which miracles may have is to demonstrate the real power of God to superstitious communities.

Once again the story demonstrates the incompatibility of Christianity and magic. In this it follows the Old Testament (Lev. 20:6; Deut. 18:10-12; Isa. 47:13-15). It also demonstrates that Jesus' power is overwhelmingly the stronger.

38 The Crippled Man Healed at Lystra
(14:8-20)

We now encounter Paul and Barnabas in the obscure and remote little town of Lystra in Lycaonia, in the mountains of what is now south central Turkey. There they find a congenitally-crippled man and, rather like Peter when he healed the crippled man at the Temple Gate (Acts 3), Paul looks at him and sees that he has faith to be healed. One can only assume that he read it in the man's eyes. The eyes are indeed the windows of the soul, and the Christian counsellor or healer today can often glean much from looking into them. The man is healed, but the pagan population react in a way that is deeply embarrassing to the two apostles: they proceed to make them objects of worship. Luke, with a kind of dry humour characteristic of him, says that they called Barnabas, Zeus, the chief of the Gods; and Paul, Hermes, because he was the one who spoke the most! The two men are appalled, rending their clothes in true Jewish style and with great difficulty dissuading the crowd from offering sacrifice to them.

It is a danger for those with a healing ministry that superstitious or pagan onlookers may attribute the healer's power to the wrong source, or think that the power resides in him or her and belongs to that person. In deterring the crowd, Paul and Barnabas preach the gospel to them, in effect, in terms that the Lycaonians will hopefully understand. This is a reminder to us that where a ministry of healing is carried out among an unbelieving or pagan population, the preaching of the Gospel or the teaching of Christian truth should never be far away, or the observers can get things badly wrong.

They discover that crowds are fickle. Some Jewish opponents of the Gospel, incensed by the apostles' activities in nearby Iconium and Antioch, come there and turn the crowd against them and Paul is actually stoned, but he miraculously gets up from the ground and with great courage goes back into the town. Later on (15:36) Paul would return, danger notwithstanding, to visit the church at Lystra, and would find a young man whom the church had produced called Timothy, who was to become his most faithful companion.

It is interesting to note that the story has some archaeological support. Bruce tells us that the archaeologist W. M. Calder discovered two Roman inscriptions at Sedasa near Lystra. One was the dedication of a statue of Hermes to Zeus by men with Lycaonian names, and the second mentioned 'priests of Zeus'. Also, Calder and Buckler discovered near Lystra an altar dedicated to 'the hearer of prayer', which might have been Zeus, and to Hermes. Of course these discoveries do not confirm the story, but they do confirm its background.

39 The Slave Girl of Philippi
(16:16-18)

Paul's journeys have at last taken him into Europe and we find him, along with his companion Silas, in Philippi, a city at the northern end of the Aegean Sea. The church he founded there gave him much joy through its generosity and maturity, as his Epistle to the Philippians indicates. But, as usual, his mission there was not without its dangers and challenges, one of which was that a slave girl kept following Paul and his companion Silas around, calling, 'These men are servants of the Most High God, who are telling you the way to be saved.'

According to the Greek, the girl was possessed by a 'Python' spirit. This has nothing to do with snakes, but links her with Delphi, a shrine where a prophetess uttered prophecies believed to be from the god Apollo. Delphi was otherwise known as Pytho. The girl would thus be regarded as a distinguished prophetess, and would bring her owners prestige and money. You might imagine that Paul and Silas welcomed this free publicity, but they did not. Paul's ability to discern spirits (see the comments on 1 Corinthians 12) would have shown him that the message was not coming from God, and he would have wanted to avoid confusion about his attitude to paganism. Besides, the girl was in need of deliverance. Paul therefore called the spirit out. After that she could no longer give prophecies, and her angry owners had Paul and Silas scourged and thrown into prison.

Peter Lawrence, an English Anglican priest, relates how he converted a woman with a history of occult involvement, with interesting results: 'Long before any demons had been cast out of her, but after she had accepted Jesus Christ as her Saviour, this lady said to me, "The power's gone. I can't do it any more. I can't read people's minds like once I could. I used to know what people were going to say before they said it, but now it's all vanished."'

The most interesting point about this story for the student of healing is that the girl was not mentally ill, so far as we can see. She exhibited no disturbing symptoms, and had she been mentally ill the debility it caused would probably have prevented her from functioning in the way she did. Often, demonised people do not present as ill at all, and this story offers biblical confirmation of that.

40 Paul's Ephesus Mission
(19:11-20)

This time we find Paul on his third 'missionary tour', in the course of which he spent more than two years at the great city of Ephesus, situated on the Aegean coast of what is now Turkey, on the opposite side of the sea from Athens. Nowadays nothing is left of Ephesus but extensive ruins, and the once-great harbour is marshland, for the city has been left high and dry. On the seashore near the city stood the huge temple of Artemis, or Diana of the Ephesians, whose statue, probably a meteorite, was said to have fallen from Heaven. Such was the impact of Paul's mission that the retail trade connected with the temple took a knock, and caused riots among the city's silversmiths.

Ephesus was also a centre of the magic arts. In those days books of magic were often called 'Ephesian scrolls'. In accordance with his usual practice in places where there was a Jewish community, Paul had begun his ministry in the synagogue; but when he encountered rejection there, he took over a lecture hall owned by one Tyrannus, who cannot have been as bad as his name suggests. The hall would have been empty during the hottest part of the afternoon, and it would be then that Paul took it over, working for the rest of the time at his trade of tent-making.

The mission was characterised by remarkable demonstrations of spiritual power, to such an extent that aprons which Paul had worn as he plied his trade, and handkerchiefs he had tied around his head to absorb the sweat, were taken and laid on sick and demonised people and they recovered. We saw earlier in this book how sick people had been placed in Peter's shadow in Jerusalem, but that it was not clear on the evidence of that passage alone that Luke approved of the practice. Here there is no doubt that he linked their recovery with the laying on of the bits of cloth from Paul's body. This raises the whole question of the role of material things in

Christian healing, but see the Byway on Objects, Substances, Shrines and Sacrament.

Ephesus being the kind of place it was, it was not long before the local magicians began to get in on the act, and it became common for exorcists to 'adjure' spirits by the name of Jesus. The way pagan exorcists operated was to call upon a spiritual power that was deemed to be more powerful than whatever had a hold of the sufferer and adjure the possessing spirit by the name of that power, which was why in the gospels some demoniacs tried to adjure Jesus in return in the attempt to gain power over him. Fragments of magical papyrus scrolls have survived, suggesting the formula, 'I adjure thee by the God of the Hebrews.' And some Jewish rabbinical writings of the time denounce a tendency for Jews to invoke the name of Jesus in healing, indicating Jesus' reputation as a mighty healer. So the story of a kind of 'travelling circus' (Professor Dunn's phrase) of wandering exorcists using the name of Jesus is true to life. Of course it does not work! The meaning of the 'name' of Jesus is dealt with in the comments on Peter and John's healing of the lame man (Acts 3), and it was made clear then that the name was very much more than a magical word.

The violence of the demoniac's response to the seven sons of Sceva's attempts to deliver him was, nevertheless, a warning that some demoniacs were dangerous and unpredictable, and this remains true at the present day. (See the Byway Demons and Deliverance.) Luke's account has about it a kind of dark humour.

The consequence is that there is an atmosphere of awe in Ephesus. Writers on religious revivals often list a sense of awe as one of the marks of a true revival. Many people are converted to Christianity, and some who are already believers bring their magical papyrus scrolls and burn them. It is not a case, note, of witches being burnt, but of witches being converted and burning their books. This move will sound drastic to some readers, but what is intended is a clean break with the past. Sometimes such a clean break with harmful influences is essential before we can go on with God.

A question raised by the story concerns the apparent inconsistency between this story and an incident recorded in Luke 9:49, 50:

' *"Master," said John, "we saw a man driving out demons in your name and we tried to stop him, because he is not one of us."*

' *"Do not stop him," Jesus said, "for whoever is not against you is for you." '*

In the gospel story, the exorcisms were apparently effective, which suggests that this was not a pagan exorcist but someone sympathetic to Jesus while operating on his own initiative. Throughout the history of the Christian Church, there have been individuals and groups who have operated in God's power outside official church structures. Many missionary societies have been founded that way, the Bible Society, The Church Missionary Society, the Franciscan Order, and so on, but these groups were far different from practitioners of magic or spiritism or whatever, wearing a Christian disguise. Jesus, with his spiritual discernment, knew the difference.

41 Eutychus at Troas
(20:7-12)

We now find Paul at Troas (Troy), situated near the Asiatic shores of the Hellespont. He is on his way to Jerusalem where he is most uncertain about his reception. (It turned out to be hostile indeed.) Perhaps because of this, he wanted to get as much teaching and wisdom across to the congregation at Troas as he possibly could. He was probably never to see them again, and might have realised it.

The little story is one of the 'we-passages' mentioned in the Introduction. It is not certain that Luke included himself in the 'we' but it is probable, and even if it isn't, what we have here is still an eye-witness account. It is also true to life. They are meeting on the first day of the week (Sunday). Many of the congregation may have been sleepy, having been at work during the day, and in addition, many oil lamps had made the chamber stuffy. Paul goes on and on (some of Luke's dry but affectionate humour here) for Paul could ramble. (He says, 'Finally, brethren . . . ' in his letter to the Philippians with half the epistle still to go!) So young Eutychus fell asleep, tumbled out of a third floor window and was taken up dead. Paul broke off his discourse and ran downstairs to him. Whether he was able to get the lad's heart going again by non-miraculous means, or whether we are talking of a miracle, we do not know, but his words in Greek are, 'Don't be afraid; his breath is in him.' It doesn't mean 'his breath is *still* in him', or the Greek would be worded differently; the young man did actually die. The matter dealt with, it was a case of going back upstairs, saying, 'Now, where was I?' and continuing with the Eucharist. There is almost a casualness about Paul's actions. In a generation of missionary service he has seen it all, and this is all in God's day's work. We are witnessing the spiritual power and authority of a man of God.

42 Healings on Malta
(28:1-10)

The immediate prequel of this narrative is a gripping account of storm and shipwreck. Paul, who is now a prisoner, has been sent from Judaea on a big grain ship to stand trial before the Emperor in Rome. Exactly what were the charges against him is difficult to establish from Luke's narrative; but the reason why he had appealed to Caesar to stand trial in Rome was probably that he wanted to establish that Christianity ('the Way' as it was then known) was a true extension of the Jewish Faith. That was because the latter was what the Romans termed a *religio licita*, i.e. a recognised religion whose devotees would not be required to burn incense to Caesar. If Paul could not demonstrate this, then Christians would not be exempted from the requirement to worship the Emperor, and because, in conscience, they would be unable to do this, persecution would inevitably follow.

None of this, of course, was known to the inhabitants of the island where the ship was wrecked following a ferocious storm, so when a serpent fastened on Paul's hand, they superstitiously assumed that he was a murderer escaped from the sea, whom justice would not allow to live. However, Paul suffered no ill effects, and Luke then drily remarks that thereupon the islanders assumed that he must be a god! There is humour in the fact that Paul and Barnabas had experienced the opposite development in Lystra. There, they had first been gods and then rogues. Here, Paul is first a rogue and then a god!

The serpent presents something of a puzzle to commentators. It is normally assumed that the island, called Melita in the Greek, was Malta. James Smith of Jordanhill, a Scottish Victorian scholar-yachtsman, claimed in 1848 that all the evidence pointed to the island's being Malta, and not, as was also claimed, the island of Melada (present-day Mljet) off the coast of Croatia. The Croatians do not buy this and still claim their island as the site of Paul's shipwreck. The thing is that poisonous snakes are found on Mljet, but not on Malta.

If we do not go for the drastic option of shifting the entire location to Mljet, various explanations are on offer. It has been suggested that there was a species of snake on Malta which was actually harmless, although it did bite and cling, but which was thought by the natives to be deadly. If this was the case, then what looks like a miracle was nothing of the kind. Luke as a doctor would have known all about snakes and their venom, and it seems a little peculiar that he did not reveal the truth about the snake but allowed the incident to look like a miracle. The other possibility is that there were indeed poisonous snakes on Malta in those days, even though there aren't any today. After all, at the time this incident took place, Scotland was inhabited by wolves, elk, lynx and wild boar!

Nearby there was an estate belonging to a man called Publius. He was the 'chief man of the island', which is not Luke's description but an official title, and, like most Roman officials in Acts, he is shown in a favourable light, for he welcomed Luke and Paul to his house. It emerged that Publius' father was seriously ill with bouts of fever and dysentery. Dr Wilkinson makes clear that this was not Malta fever, which is actually brucellosis, but acute bacillary dysentery. According to Sir William Ramsay, the language Luke uses is medical rather than popular, further confirmation that it was indeed Luke who was the eye-witness present with Paul.

Paul lays hands on the old man after prayer, the classic healing procedure; but it may be that Paul did not do this because it was 'standard', but rather that the guidance to lay on hands in this case came as a result of the prayer. The verse is a gentle reminder of the importance of prayer in the healing ministry. The patient is healed, and although the healing was possibly not public, all the rest of the islanders come with their diseases and are cured.

What we make of verse 9 is more important than a first glance would suggest. Luke was a doctor. Did he ignore his medicine and resort entirely to prayer and the laying on of hands? And did he always do that at that time, having laid his medicine aside? Paul, however, at about this time of his life, wrote of him to the Colossians, describing him as 'beloved physician', as if he still plied his trade. This suggests that Luke combined medicine with prayer; in which case he probably did so on this occasion. This little episode therefore lends biblical support to the idea of co-operation between pastor and doctor.

section 4

A tour of other important passages

Preliminary briefing

At the end of this book you will not have visited all the 'healing passages' in the Bible, though you will have visited all the healing stories. A list of other passages is given in the Appendix, all of them being worth a read.

What follows now is a selection of passages with important things to say about healing. Selections like these are always made in the light of what the commentator thinks is important, and someone else would have chosen differently. At the same time there is an inevitability about most of the passages chosen here.

43 'The Spirit of the Lord is upon me' – Luke 4:16-21
44 The Wounded Healer. Matthew – 8:16, 17
45 The Wholeness of the Person – 1 Thessalonians 5:23, 24
46 The Maintenance of Inner Health – Philippians 4:4-7
47 The Role of Holy Communion – 1 Corinthians 11:23-26
48 The Thorn in the Flesh – 2 Corinthians 12:7-10
49 The Gifts of the Spirit – 1 Corinthians 12:1-13, 27-31
50 Anointing and the Prayer of Faith – James 5:14-16

43 'The Spirit of the Lord is upon me'
(Luke 4:16-21)

This passage forms part of a longer story of how Jesus preached in his home town of Nazareth, but was rejected by the townspeople. Mark (6:1-6) and Matthew (13:54-58) tell the same tale but with three differences:

• they do not tell us what Jesus said to the synagogue congregation,
• they place the incident at a later point in Jesus' career, and
• they do not say anything about Jesus' being driven out of town.

There is evidence in Luke 4:23 that this event did not occur right at the beginning of Jesus' ministry, for Jesus had done some teaching and healing in Galilee already, but Luke places the incident at the start of Jesus' ministry in order to put everything in context and explain what is coming.

Luke says that Jesus went to the synagogue on the Sabbath, which he was accustomed to do. Synagogues were actually quite a new idea at that time, and were basically centres of teaching. An interesting thing about this passage is that it is actually the earliest known description of synagogue worship. We do not go looking for other descriptions of synagogue services in order to illuminate this story. We look at this story to find out about synagogue services! However, from this and later descriptions we learn that the service would probably have consisted firstly of prayers, which would include the prayer called the *Shema* (Deuteronomy 6:1-9). Then there would be a reading from the books of the Law, which would be specified, like in the lectionary used by the Christian Church today; and this would be followed by a reading from the prophets which was chosen by the reader. Readings would be in the original Hebrew, but a translation into Aramaic would be given. Then, having stood up to read, out of respect for the Word of God, the reader would sit down and give a sermon. We have already seen how that sermon would cite the authority of other rabbis, but Jesus spoke on his own authority, with electrifying effect.

That his ministry began with teaching is once again a reminder to us that we cannot separate out the ministry of healing, or other good works for that matter, from preaching the Gospel and teaching about the Christian faith. Even as people without faith witness Christians living an intriguingly different life characterised by love and joy, sometimes by remarkable things happening, they need to know what it is all about and how they themselves might attain it.

So Jesus spoke on the prophet Isaiah 61:1, 2, with a piece included from Isaiah 58:6:

'The Spirit of the Sovereign Lord is on me, because the Lord has anointed me to preach good news to the poor. He has sent me to bind up the broken-hearted, to proclaim freedom for the captives and release from darkness for the prisoners, to proclaim the year of the Lord's favour.'

Jesus tells his hearers that something like Jubilee year has arrived (the year of the Lord's favour), Jubilee year being the one year in every fifty when slaves could be released, land returned to its original owners, fields lie fallow, and debts be forgiven (Leviticus 25:8-54). At this time, people are to be not just *literally* released from prison and from blindness, but also *metaphorically*, because, as John's Gospel teaches, people can be spiritually blind as well as physically blind. It is also true that people with freedom to come and go as they please may nevertheless be prisoners of all kinds of anger, bitterness, fear, insecurity, doubt or rage. Some manuscripts of the passage add, 'to bind up the broken-hearted', and if they are authentic we also have here a mandate for 'inner healing': the healing of sicknesses of the soul as well as the body.

Jesus says that to enable him to proclaim all these various forms of 'release' he has been anointed with the Holy Spirit of God, who is God living and working through human beings. Luke described Christ's 'anointing' in the previous chapter, when Jesus went to John the Baptist to be baptised. He had no need to be baptised, being a pure, sinless human being, and baptism signified repentance, but he went through the baptism because he wished to identify himself with people in every way (see the following section), and it was as he did this that the Spirit came upon him. We learn from this that if Jesus, the Son of God, needed the Spirit to fulfil his calling, how much more do we! And that it was as he *identified* himself with the sinful and the needy that the anointing came.

The story goes on to tell how Jesus sought to explain the apparent failure of his ministry in Nazareth. No mighty works had happened because of their unbelief, and sometimes it happens that a prophet lacks honour among his own people. People who live in small closely-knit communities do often take a dim view of someone from among them who achieves fame and fortune or rises above his or her station. 'We kent his faither,' as the Scots might say. In this case it was this attitude that lay behind their unbelief. They could not believe that the carpenter's lad could be a prophet, let alone the Messiah, and this explained not only the absence of miracles in Nazareth, but also the murderous opposition which rose to the surface eventually and made them drive him out of town.

44 The Wounded Healer
(Matthew 8:16, 17)

This small but mighty passage has parallels in Mark (1:29-34) and in Luke (4:38-41), and is one of the many 'summary statements' about healings in the first three gospels (see Appendix) which, taken together, give an impression of healings happening on a vast scale, and the streets of Capernaum or the hills of Galilee teeming with needy humanity. The reason for picking out this passage from the many we could have chosen is the importance of the quotation from the Old Testament, which only Matthew includes. It is one of many Old Testament quotes scattered all through his gospel with the object of helping the reader see how Jesus fulfilled the Old Testament. Sometimes it is not immediately obvious why Matthew has picked a particular passage, but often when we reflect on it the meaning begins to 'click'.

The words, 'He took up our infirmities and carried our sorrows' come from Isaiah 53:4, in which the prophet tells of a mysterious, lonely, despised, suffering character who is eventually scourged and killed, but whose suffering in some way brings forgiveness and healing: the so-called 'Suffering Servant'. Lovers of classical music will be familiar with the chorus from Handel's *Messiah*, which goes, 'Surely he hath borne our griefs and carried our sorrows', and is a setting of the same verse. There were many versions of the Old Testament or of particular passages from it available to the early Christians, and Matthew's version of this verse doesn't talk about 'griefs and sorrows' but 'infirmities and diseases'.

At the heart of Christianity, not just its teaching on healing, lies the idea that God has always been three in one (the Trinity), the three being Father, Son, and Holy Spirit, and that God the Son became the man Jesus of Nazareth, who experienced all that life can throw at human beings. He *identified* himself with humanity, going through the experiences that we go through. In the Epistle to the Hebrews, one of the New Testament epistles, Jesus is likened to a high priest. The function of priests is to bring God to people and people to God; and the qualification for bringing people to God is that, like Moses and Aaron (Psalm 90), we are identified with the people on whose behalf we come before him. Jesus is our great High Priest, but we Christians are also a priesthood (1 Peter 2:5), and, insofar as we, too, are identified with the needy people that we pray for, our prayers have power with God, and healing follows.

In 1904 a great religious revival swept through the Welsh valleys, bringing thousands of people to Christian faith, and transforming their lives and the lives of scores of communities. One village in the hills above Swansea remained untouched by the revival, however, and it was a community in great need. Poverty, TB and drunkenness were rife. In a village not far away lived a group of Christians whose leading light was a young man called Rees Howells. Not long converted, Howells had nevertheless allowed himself to be 'taught of God' right from the start, and had matured rapidly into a spiritual giant who was to go on in later years to be an outstandingly effective missionary and man of prayer.

Howells and his companions were concerned that the nearby village should experience revival, but they appear to have understood right from the start that merely to pray about the community from outside would not be sufficient, and neither would a hit-and-run approach of occasional contact with its members. Instead, having worked by day as miners, hacking away at the hard Welsh anthracite, they would don ordinary working clothes, so as to be identified with the villagers, and walk over the hills to the needy community, where they would visit the people, pray with them, do what they could to meet their material needs, and simply identify with them. After they had done that for some time, revival came to that village too. Costly identification was needed, and we see this first in Jesus as he served the needy people of Capernaum.

Many contemporary writers on healing speak of the need to be identified with the sufferer. In the course of the research which led to this book, I frequently encountered the idea of *The Wounded Healer*. It is actually a title of a book by Henri Nouwen, who gave up a distinguished academic career to work tirelessly among handicapped people. It does appear that such identification is a qualification for an effective healing ministry.

45 The Wholeness of the Human Being
(1 Thessalonians 5:23, 24)

I shall set this short passage out in full to save you the job of looking it up.

'May God himself, the God of peace, sanctify you through and through. May your whole spirit, soul and body be kept blameless at the coming of our Lord Jesus Christ. The one who calls you is faithful and he will do it.'

Paul often refers to God as 'the God of peace'. Does he mean by this the God of *Shalom*, or something different? This is a question examined in the last section of this book. However we answer that question, it is clear what Paul seeks in his prayer for the Thessalonians. He wants them to be holy, which means a state of being 'set apart for God' and which shows itself in the character. A good description of holiness is to be found elsewhere in Paul's writings in Galatians 5:22, 23:

'The fruit of the Spirit is love, joy, peace, patience, kindness, goodness, faithfulness, gentleness and self-control.'

To live a life characterised by that list of virtues is a tall order, in fact, humanly speaking, quite impossible, but Paul says with emphasis that it is *God* who does the work of making us holy. We cannot do it ourselves, and our only role is to put ourselves in the place where we allow God to enter our personality, sort us out and fill us with the love, joy and peace, and so on. That place is on our knees in prayer. But there is no uncertainty about the answer to that prayer. 'He is faithful,' says Paul, 'and he will do it.'

Some writers identify holiness with wholeness, that is, *shalom*, but there is no indication in the New Testament that they are the same thing by different names. They do need to be distinguished. But though they should be distinguished, they cannot be separated. The tractor and the trailer are two different things, but they go together, and are useless without each other. Many people are not whole because they are not holy, and many are not holy because they are not whole. And even when a holy personality can be found in a broken body, the weakness of the body may prevent the sick person from fulfilling God's call, unless healing for the body can be found.

That thought brings us to another noteworthy feature of this passage. Paul asks that our 'spirit, soul and body' may be kept blameless at the coming of the Lord Jesus. Most commentators on this verse say that when Paul refers to spirit, soul and body it is only his way of saying, 'may our *whole selves* be kept blameless and holy.' I am not at all sure of that. Paul is not implying 'we can be *thought of* sometimes as a soul, sometimes as a spirit and sometimes as a body'; he is implying that we *consist of* the three components.

So we can distinguish the three, and we sometimes need to, but they are nevertheless a unity, and should not be separated. It is important to remember this when we consider healing, for often what goes on in the mind (or, if you like, the soul) affects what goes on in the body, and vice versa. Some years ago something appeared to be wrong with me spiritually. I had no appetite for life or for worship, could not care less whether my flock was properly cared for or whether or not anyone was converted. There was no joy in me, there was internal turmoil rather than peace, and a serious lack of the energy to take an interest in other people or to do the things that loving them demanded. Friends noticed this and concluded that I had a spiritual problem. I even thought so myself. Then I was diagnosed as having a seriously underactive thyroid gland. I was put on thyroxin tablets, and the problem gradually cleared up. When health returned, holiness became possible.

The process can work in the opposite direction too. Lack of holy living can cause a lack of health. The late Dr Bob Lambourne, a pioneer of Holistic medicine, wrote: 'Envy, hatred and malice can change the structure of the lining of a man's stomach, alter the clotting of the blood and – indeed through the hypothalamus and vegetative nervous system emotional changes in the person bring observable changes in every part of the body.'

Some of Lambourne's medical terminology may be lost on us, but we get the idea. Lambourne was not alone in his opinions. Dr Morton Kelsey has pointed out how tuberculosis is more likely to flare up in certain personalities than in others, and the healer Esmond Jefferies talks at length in his book *The Power and the Glory* about links between cancers and the patient's state of mind. It follows that healing and sanctification (the process of making us holy) are bound up with each other; that holiness may bring a person health, or alternatively healing may be necessary before a holy life can be lived. This is not always the case, and we have also to recognise that sometimes it is only through bodily weakness that we are motivated to keep in touch with God. (See the comments on Paul's 'thorn in the flesh' below). We are all different, and often a person will need healing of some kind before she can be holy. Proverbs 17:22 bears all this out when it says, 'A cheerful heart is good medicine, but a crushed spirit dries up the bones.'

These verses also bring home to us that the New Testament

teaching on healing is not just about healing miracles as such. Often physical healing comes only when one's attitudes or relationships get sorted out. Chaplains, priests and sick visitors know that helping patients to tidy up their lives, attitudes, habits and relationships, in the power of God and under the guidance of his Word, can have an incalculably positive effect on their recovery.

One last important point. It is holiness that is the most important thing. God does not exist to serve our need for a sense of well-being so that we can go on living a happy but self-centred life. We exist to serve *him*. Healing is a means to that end. It isn't an end in itself.

46 The Maintenance of Inner Health
(Philippians 4:4-7)

Most of what we have looked at so far has had to do with how health of body or soul is *created*, but the passage before us now has to do with how health of soul, inner health, is *maintained*. Nowadays we apply rules of hygiene to defend our bodies from poisoning or infection, but Paul's words here indicate how one can practise *mental* hygiene. The words come across all the more convincingly if we realise that Paul is in Rome (following the journey on which he was shipwrecked), and in prison or under house arrest, with an uncertain future. The staggering thing is that an epistle written in jail by a writer chained to two Roman soldiers should be so full of joy, confidence and optimism. The experience of prison has not poisoned or affected Paul's mind, and the passage in front of us makes clear how he prevented it from doing so. He gives several pieces of advice, and then tells us the consequences of following them:

❏ *Rejoice!* Look for the good things about whatever situation you find yourself in. Such things can always be found, and when you find them, celebrate them by what you say and sing. 'Let the glory out', as an old chorus puts it. 'Praise,' wrote C. S. Lewis, 'is inner health made audible.' So we are to rejoice; but that rejoicing should be 'in the Lord'. It is best to celebrate in worship, rather than in 'going down the pub'!

❏ *Let your gentleness be evident to all.* The word translated 'gentleness' is *epieikes.* It would be fine if every word in New Testament Greek had an exact equivalent in English and vice versa, but unfortunately that often isn't the case, and it isn't here. We cannot put the word exactly into English. It clearly means a rather lovely human trait, but what? Karl Barth, the great Swiss theologian, in his famous commentary on the Epistle to the Philippians, puts it this way: 'It is your quite specifically-grounded benevolence, gentleness, considerateness, openness, vitality and at the same time moderation – that must become manifest to all men.' 'Graciousness' would be another close translation, or, as the writer Ernest Hemingway once put it, 'grace under pressure'. Once again we have to let it out. Just as tea or coffee left in the pot and never poured out becomes cold and rancid, so pleasure or graciousness bottled up and not shared goes off. When Paul says, 'The Lord is near', he does not mean that the Lord is close to us when we pray, though that is true. He means that the Lord will come again soon, so our trials will soon be over.

❏ *Do not be anxious about anything.* Many people, though they may be sincere Christians, lack a sense of what is known in theology as the 'providence' of God. For such people, life is pretty random, and they conduct themselves as if they must take care of their own circumstances, because if they don't, no one else will, and neither will God, who is too big and too far away to be bothered with their little needs. And when such people cannot take care of their circumstances, they worry. The answer to this anxiety is for them to remind themselves regularly that they have a God who 'in all things works for the good of those who love him' (Romans 8:28), and who is concerned to know what is on his children's minds so that he can help them.

❏ *Prayer and petition.* This is not a repetition of two words which mean the same thing. For many people, prayer simply means asking. (God, give me . . . give me . . . give me . . . Amen.) But there is much more to prayer than that. It can mean saying sorry to God (penitence); it can mean just being quiet before God and listening; it can mean thanking him, or bringing him questions and perplexities, and so on. Yet it does involve asking for quite specific things, as well. Present your requests to God, says Paul, and that might mean more papyrus to write on, more comfortable shackles, safe passage for a friend, or what have you. Many prayers, especially prayers that are read, are rather general, with the result that we do not know whether God has said 'yes' to them or not. Specific prayers can be scary, but they have an advantage. You know if and when they have been answered, and that builds up your faith, because if prayer has been answered in a rather wonderful and obvious way once, you can believe that it will happen again.

❏ *With thanksgiving.* Thanksgiving is a key Christian attitude and one that we can choose to adopt. Thanksgiving is praise made specific. It is also the opposite of grumbling! The grumbler goes into a situation and spells out to himself what is wrong with the situation, its drawbacks, and who should be blamed for them, etc., and then feels bad about it. The thankful person, on the other hand, going into a similar situation, spells out what is good and positive about it, what possibilities and advantages it has, and then praises God for it. Christians are not so much thankful because they're joyful as joyful because they're thankful. If we make a habit of obeying these rules of mental hygiene, there will be a consequence: *the peace of God* will guard our hearts and minds in Christ Jesus.

In the Old Testament survey in the Introduction, *shalom* (peace) was described. The peace of God mentioned here is something rather different. *Shalom* was a sense of well-being that had a lot to do with a person's circumstances: family, prosperity, health, relationships and so on. The peace mentioned here has very little to do with one's circumstances, and is best described as inner peace: a sense of serenity and calm at the heart of the personality, which can persist even through severe trouble. It is said to transcend all understanding, because an inner peace which endures despite horrendous outer circumstances does take some understanding. And yet, that is God's gift to Christians. 'Peace I leave with you. Not as the world gives do I give to you,' said Jesus. In the list of 'fruit of the Spirit' in Galatians 5:22, 23, peace comes third in the list, after joy, to which it is closely akin. An old Scottish theologian once wrote that 'Peace is joy resting and joy is peace dancing', a wonderful picture of the relationship between the two.

But this peace is not just a good feeling, helpful though good feelings may be. It has an active role in maintaining the Christian's inner health. In 2 Corinthians 11:32, 33, Paul gives his readers a fragment of autobiography. He tells how, shortly after his dramatic conversion on the road to Damascus, and his beginning to preach the Gospel in that city, he must have got into trouble, because the governor of the city had the city gate guarded in order to arrest him (he escaped by being lowered down the walls in a basket). The point is that the Greek word he used of the soldiers 'guarding' the city was the same as the word he uses here of the peace of God guarding the heart and the mind. The picture is of a personality that could so easily be invaded by the poison and infection of fear and anxiety, hate and prejudice, depression and horror, but which is defended by peace, like a garrison of soldiers defending a city.

Elsewhere, in his epistle to the Colossians (3:15), Paul tells his readers to let the peace of Christ 'rule' in their hearts. Here a different word is used, and the suggestion seems to be not only that the heart is subject to invasion by all kinds of negative and destructive thoughts, but that there can also be, as it were, 'civil disorder', with the heart in turmoil, and different thoughts and attitudes – some good, some bad – warring with one another. Here, the peace is not so much like a regiment guarding the personality from invasion from outside as a police force keeping order within.

All too many of us badly need a healthy heart and mind, indeed, a whole personality, if we are to be free to help and serve others, and to help them find healing in turn. We need, as an old hymn says:

> A heart at leisure from itself
> To soothe and sympathise.

Paul here points the way to the inner peace which maintains the heart at leisure from itself.

Objects, Substances, Shrines and Sacrament

Some Christians set a lot of store by healing through objects such as relics of the saints, or by visiting healing shrines, so it is important to see what light the New Testament can shed on such things.

Basically, there are four attitudes towards them that can be taken:

1) They are efficacious in themselves, regardless of the attitude or moral or spiritual state of the sufferer.
2) They may at times be efficacious in themselves, but only when accompanied by the right attitude (particularly faith).
3) They are not efficacious in themselves, but may have some value as an aid to faith.
4) They are of no value and should be avoided, because of the risk of superstition.

Of these four attitudes, the first should certainly be avoided, being characteristic of magic. More surprisingly, however, the opposite extreme, number four, cannot be sustained from the New Testament either, because the grasping of Jesus' cloak by the woman with the haemorrhage (Mark 5:25 and parallels) and by others (Mark 6:53-56; Matthew 14:34-36); the anointing with oil engaged in by the disciples (Mark 6:13) and recommended by James (5:14-16); the shadow of Peter (Acts 5:15, 16), and the cloths taken from the body of Paul (Acts 19:11, 12), all suggest that particular objects or actions may from time to time be a means of healing. However, there are certain things that we need to bear firmly in mind:

- The use of objects is usually peculiar to a particular time and place, and not to be universally applied. Back in the Old Testament, Numbers 21:6-9 tells how the Israelites, wandering in the Wilderness of Sinai, were afflicted by a plague of serpents, so Moses erected a bronze serpent so that the people could look at it and be healed. Astonishingly, we read in 2 Kings 18:4 that the bronze serpent still existed hundreds of years later, and had to be destroyed by the reforming King Hezekiah because the semi-pagan Israelites were worshipping it!

- The object or substance would be effective only if the Holy Spirit had guided the healer to use it at a particular time. Jesus used spittle or clay on some occasions, but usually he did not.

- It is still *God* who does the healing through the *faith* of the sufferer or the sufferer's friends. In the case of the woman with the haemorrhage, all the evangelists report that Jesus said to her, 'Your faith has saved you.' The attitude was important, even though Jesus was aware that power had flowed out of him. In the passage in James 5, oil is to be used, certainly, but it is 'the prayer of faith' which will save the sick person; while in Acts 19:11, 12, we are told that *God* did extraordinary miracles by the hands of Paul. So it is God, not the object or substance, who does the healing, and though his power may flow through a substance, or accompany the use of a substance (I'm not sure which) it does need to connect with faith. If we liken the Holy Spirit to electricity, then, just as electricity will flow into certain substances but not others, in the same way the Holy Spirit needs to be connected to the living water of faith, not the solid rubber of unbelief.

What are we to make of the ministry of healing shrines, like Walsingham or Knock, Mediugorje or Lourdes? Here there is certainly a danger that a kind of magical belief in the effectiveness of the waters may develop, especially in the minds of unsophisticated and needy people. Some years ago I talked with Father Peter Walter of the Anglican shrine at Walsingham, who seemed well aware of this risk, and spoke of how counselling now plays an important part in the sanctuary's ministry. Nowadays the confessional has a door leading off it into a counselling room, while the shrine's collection of relics are tucked discreetly away in a cupboard. Father Walter also spoke of how Walsingham had become a place where 'prayer had been valid' (quoting the poet T. S. Eliot). Shrines and places of pilgrimage certainly seem often to be locales where God is powerfully present (as if there is a permanent anointing), and this may be because, although we must not forget that God is present and available to us everywhere, there may still be places where he has 'made his name to dwell'. On the other hand, it

> may simply be that the place with all its associations has become an aid to faith for purely psychological reasons, which may not be a bad thing.
>
> If we think that there is enough evidence to justify our believing that objects are effective in healing when Spirit–guided and linked to faith, then Holy Communion must have a power way beyond its undoubted psychological effects, for here we have an act, involving substances, which is not just commanded for a particular occasion but for all time.
>
> So, a magical view of substances and objects is to be avoided at one extreme, but so too is an attitude that rejects them out of hand. They may, as God directs, be vehicles of his power, and on other occasions they may still, with all their associations, be aids to faith.

47 The Role of Holy Communion
(1 Corinthians 11:23-26)

Holy Communion is an enormous subject. The rite, known variously as Mass, Communion, The Lord's Supper, Breaking of Bread, or Eucharist, lies right at the heart of Christian worship. This is not the place to give an account of how it has developed over the centuries, the debates about it that have taken place, and all that it means for Christians. All I can hope to do is give a brief account, based on what Paul says about it in his first letter to the Corinthians, of its meaning, with special reference to healing.

This is the earliest account we have of how Jesus instituted Communion, because in all probability 1 Corinthians was written before any of the gospels. The wording is strongly reminiscent of Luke's account of Jesus' words at the last supper he had with his disciples on the night before he died, which tells us that the material was handed down by word of mouth for a period before it was written up by the Gospel writers. Paul himself says as much in verse 23.

The meaning of Communion can be summed up in five ideas: Fellowship, Thanksgiving, Covenant, Remembrance, and Anticipation.

Fellowship
Paul has earlier said in his letter (10:15-17) how the bread, which is taken and broken and shared, symbolises the fact that Christians are one body, the body of Christ. A Christian document of the second century called the 'Didache' ('The Teaching of the Twelve Apostles') gives a full description of the Communion as it was celebrated in those days. Apparently, in the prayer of thanksgiving which was offered before the bread and wine were shared, God was thanked that the bread that had once been seed that was scattered on the ground had now grown up, been gathered and turned into bread. Then a prayer was offered that in the same way God's Church might be gathered into his Kingdom from the ends of the Earth.

But Paul has a particular reason for reminding the Corinthians of how the Communion service was instituted. This was in the very earliest days of the Christian Church, before the service had developed into a ritual where Christians receive a symbolic sip of wine and a wafer or small piece of bread. In Corinth it was still very much a meal, and was treated in much the same way as the Christians there would have approached banqueting, before they were converted to Christianity.

The *triclinium*, or dining room, of even the grandest Roman houses did not seat more than twenty people at most, so the people who were deemed to be most important dined there, while the also-rans were fed elsewhere, usually in the *atrium*, on inferior food. If the also-rans were late, the banquet would go ahead without them. To make matters worse, the drinks that would follow the meal were an opportunity for some people to get drunk. Paul sternly condemned all this. The people, he said, needed to discern that they were part of a Body in which these old social distinctions no longer applied, and they needed to conduct themselves with respect and reverence, because this was an awesome event. We can all be invited to the feast, and that is all down to God's grace, because no one is worthy, but we need to conduct ourselves in a worthy *manner* when we are there.

We still need to remember this in our own day, because Communion means togetherness or fellowship. The primary significance of this for healing is that there are people in every community and every church who perhaps have no family of their own, who are prone to a disease of the soul called loneliness, with the lack of a sense of identity and belonging that goes along with it. Such people should be brought to a Communion service, and there given a warm welcome, and helped to see that though they may have nowhere else to belong and no one to whom to belong, yet they belong to Christ and are part of his family.

Thanksgiving
Nowadays, 'Communion' is the most common term for the service in Protestant Christianity, but in the early days of the Church its name was the Eucharist, which is Greek for thanksgiving. Paul speaks of 'the cup of thanksgiving for which we give thanks' in the Communion service, and very early in its history the thanksgiving extended into a lengthy prayer. Methodist Communion services in the UK contain, as do other liturgies, a 'great prayer of thanksgiving', in which we thank and praise God for all he has done for us in creating us and saving us from our sins. Thanksgiving, as we saw in the previous section, is an essential part of the healing of the soul, transforming grumbling, or bitterness or negativity into a joyful, positive outlook, which has its effect not only upon our souls but also on our bodies, for it can also be shown how the body is benefited or harmed, depending on our attitude.

Covenant

When, at that last supper, Jesus took the goblet of wine which was traditionally drunk at the close of a Jewish meal, he said, 'This cup is the New Covenant in my blood.' We met the Old and New Covenants in our 'reconnaissance' of the Old Testament. Under the Old, Israel had to keep God's commands, and if they did so they would be blessed both materially and spiritually, but if they failed, they would be cursed. In the event they failed repeatedly to keep the Covenant; but Jeremiah the prophet saw that one day a new Covenant would be inaugurated.

The effect of Jesus' death on the Cross was to reconcile people to God. It was as if a barrier between human beings and their Maker had been torn down, like the curtain in the Temple (Matthew 27:51). After that, the healing power of the Holy Spirit could flow into believers, and bring with it renewal. This reconciliation made it possible for the New Covenant to come into effect.

Christians do not normally steal things from supermarkets, and this is not because there are cameras and security people around, and they would go to jail if apprehended. There might be no security measure in place whatsoever, and it would still not occur to them to steal. This is because they have the 'law within' and do not need the 'law outside'. Moreover, as they walk with God it becomes increasingly the case that they feel love spontaneously, and react naturally to things in a Christian way. They no longer need the blessings and curses of the Old Covenant because their hearts have been renewed. With that renewal comes a measure of inner healing. A divided heart is a place of stress; a unified heart is a place of peace and wholeness.

Remembrance

It was common for distinguished Greeks, like the philosopher Epicurus, to set aside money in their wills for memorial meals to be held in their honour after their death. Perhaps the nearest equivalent in our experience is the Burns' Supper, in honour of Scottish poet Robert Burns. According to some commentators it was something like this that Jesus had in mind when he instituted the Lord's Supper. The great Swiss Reformer Ulrich Zwingli (1484-1531) taught that the Communion service was simply a memorial service for Jesus. Memorial services can be very moving, depending on how much the remembered one was loved and respected, yet their effect may be purely emotional, psychological and human; there need be nothing mystical or supernatural there.

Paul, however, taught that there was more to Communion than that. Just as there were kinds of sacrifices offered at the Temple that involved the family offering the sacrifice sitting down together and partaking of the meat from the sacrifice, so when we come to the Communion we take the life of God into us (10:18-21). Paul does not say so in so many words, but it goes without saying that when Communion is taken worthily and sincerely, it will have a profoundly healing effect on the participants.

A chaplain was giving a teaching course at the Old Rectory Crowhurst, England, a healing centre which puts Communion at the centre of its life, and he recalled how the medical staff at his hospital showed surprise at the progress of certain patients. 'What have you done to them?' asked a doctor. 'They received Communion,' was the reply.

Anticipation

But the rite does not only look back; it also looks forward, not to anything in this world, but to a time when Jesus will have come again, and he, and we, will join in the greatest party of all. Belief in life after death is basic to Christianity. Later on in 1 Corinthians 15, Paul says that if there is no resurrection from the dead 'we are to be pitied more than all men.' Communion brings healing in this area too. When we have fellowship together at the Lord's table, we have fellowship not only with those who are still around in the flesh, walking life's way with us, but also with the Christians of all generations. This can be a comfort for those in the throes of grief.

The belief in an afterlife frees us to live a life of self-sacrifice in this world. If this life were the only one of which I could be certain, then my concern might be to gain as much joy and gladness for myself as I possibly could while still here. The effect of this would be to make me selfish and anxious. If, however, I know that the real bliss and joy awaits me in the next life, I can hold this life and its enjoyments loosely. This doesn't make me 'so heavenly-minded I'm no earthly good'; it does the opposite. It sets me free from selfishness and anxiety to be a healing influence, bringing *shalom* into the lives of others.

All these things are wrapped up in Holy Communion.

48 The Thorn in the Flesh
(2 Corinthians 12:7-10)

If we pray for someone's healing and it does not happen, why might this be? Wisdom suggests a number of reasons:

❑ The illness may be one which would respond well to medical treatment, and it is God's will that we should (normally) seek such treatment. The prayer is then answered by means of medicine, which is also a gift of God.

❑ The sufferer may be elderly, and it is best for them that their earthly sufferings should be ended. For a Christian, death may be the ultimate healing – that is, death by natural causes, in God's time.

❑ The condition may be the result of a bad habit, like smoking, overeating or sexual misbehaviour, and healing is withheld until the person's habits are sorted out.

❑ The condition presented for healing may not be the matter that most needs healing in that person's life. There may be a root cause which the sufferer is unwilling to face, but, until that cause is dealt with, healing of the condition would be short-lived or impossible. Sometimes a person may suffer from a tangle of medical, emotional and relationship problems, in which the medical problem cannot be dealt with until something more basic is sorted out. For instance a woman's chest problem may not be solved unless she gives up smoking, but she may feel unable to do so because smoking helps her to cope with the stress of an abusive relationship which she is afraid to come out of.

But there are often cases where no such explanations seem to apply. The well-known English preacher David Watson died of cancer at the age of fifty, despite world-wide prayers for him and ministry from Morris Maddocks and John Wimber. Watson was himself a man of great faith. His death caused concern and controversy in certain Christian circles, because many believers thought that in those circumstances it ought not to have happened. It does appear that healing is withheld from some people for reasons that are not fully understood.

This was perhaps how it was for the apostle Paul, for in the passage before us he speaks of having 'a thorn in the flesh, a messenger of Satan to torment' him; and three times he pleaded with God in vain for its removal. A lot of ink, sweat and coffee have been expended by commentators in the effort to establish what the 'thorn' actually was. It is quite possible that it was not an illness at all. It is unlikely that it was a habitual sin on Paul's part, because it is beyond belief that God would refuse to deliver him from that. It is just possible that it was a besetting temptation, however, which Paul was normally able to overcome in God's strength, but which was always there. It is also possible that the thorn was something outside of Paul altogether. The Greek version of the Old Testament, known as the Septuagint (usually indicated by the Roman numerals LXX in scholarly works), translates Numbers 33:55 like this:

'If you do not drive out the inhabitants of the land, those you allow to remain will become barbs in your eyes and thorns in your sides.'

So it is possible that by the thorn in the flesh Paul meant an individual or group of people who were hostile to him. It is known that at one stage in his career he had an enemy called Alexander the coppersmith (2 Timothy 4:14), and there were certainly others. However, the way the Greek is worded in verse 9 of the passage before us suggests that not only had the thorn not been removed; it was never going to be. Enemies can be destroyed or won over, or turn their attentions elsewhere. So the illness theory seems to be the most likely explanation, even if there is no way of being certain.

But if the thorn was an illness, what kind of illness was it? Here, there seem to be as many theories as commentators! Malaria is suggested by Dr Wilkinson. Acute ophthalmia is another suggestion. But we really do not know, and perhaps do not need to know, so long as we accept that Paul's illness was chronic, recurring and debilitating, and it wasn't going to be taken away.

In a sense, too, it does not even matter whether the thorn was an illness or some other source of suffering. The point was that Paul was left with the problem to keep him from becoming proud; and also because in his weakness he was more likely to draw on God's strength. The significance for us is that God may not remove from us the hardships we ask him to remove, whether illness or something else, because the thing we most need is holiness of life. Holiness may be promoted by a sense of well-being and being set free from various illnesses of body or soul, but then again, depending on the person's personality and circumstances, it may just as often be promoted by hardship. We are all different, and for one person holiness may not be achievable unless a hardship or illness is removed, while, for another, holiness would not be achievable unless he or she had to learn through hardship or weakness to draw on the strength of God.

Clearly, this explains why God sometimes says 'no' to our prayers for an illness to be removed. The problem remains of how in such circumstances we are to exercise faith for healing.

How are we to trust God in any particular case if we don't know whether or not he intends healing?

We need, first of all, to pray for guidance. What is God doing or about to do here? As we grow in spiritual maturity, the clearer will be our ability to discern God's guidance, both as to whether or not he is going to heal someone, and when and how he is going to do it. There is evidence that Jesus himself had to do this too:

'I tell you the truth, the Son can do nothing by himself; he can do only what he sees his Father doing, because whatever the Father does the Son also does. For the Father loves the Son and shows him all he does.' John 5:19, 20.

The Holy Spirit's Work

The Holy Spirit is 'God in action', particularly in the lives of people. The ministry of healing has to be exercised in his power. (I say 'his' not 'its' power, because the Holy Spirit is the third *person* of the Godhead.) We have already pointed out in the Introductory Section on the Old Testament how the Holy Spirit is not found in everyone, but has to be consciously invited into one's life. Part of that process is repentance (Acts 2:38) and, as that verse says, baptism in water is involved too.

Yet it is difficult to generalise about how the Holy Spirit comes and how he works. Meteorologists in the twenty-first century are still uncertain in their predictions of how the winds will behave, especially in a maritime climate like that of the British Isles, and likewise the Spirit's work cannot altogether be predicted (John 3:8). We can only speak of how he 'tends' to work, and this needs to be borne in mind in what follows.

People 'receive' the Holy Spirit when they make their own decision to put their trust in Christ, repent of their sin and follow him. The reception of the Spirit is a conscious experience, and it is by virtue of receiving the Spirit that the new Christian knows that he or she belongs to God, has in effect been adopted as God's child, and will, if he or she does not renounce the Faith, go to Heaven (2 Corinthians 5:4, 5). It is as if our 'adoption certificate' is the Holy Spirit.

But the Spirit's work in the believer's life is far from ending there. There is much more to be done. It is common for Christians in certain traditions, such as Pentecostalism, to talk about 'baptism in the Spirit', and by this they mean a second experience of the Holy Spirit's coming into their lives, and thereby putting them on a whole new level of power, ability and freedom to exercise the gifts of the Spirit (see next section). It may, however, be the case that in the New Testament this term refers only to the first great filling with the Holy Spirit which the apostles experienced at the Jewish feast of Pentecost (Acts 1:5). That was a momentous historic occasion and marked the birth of Christianity. Perhaps, therefore, the term 'baptism in the Spirit' should be reserved only for that event.

The New Testament also talks of 'receiving' the Holy Spirit, 'having' the Holy Spirit, being 'full' of the Spirit or being 'filled' with him, and of the Holy Spirit 'falling upon' believers. It appears that all Christians have *received* the Holy Spirit, but not all of them are necessarily *full* of him. Paul tells the Christians at Ephesus to 'be filled with the Spirit' (Ephesians 5:18), for this is what the Greek of that verse means. It is as if we can be likened to water jugs which are filled up and poured out, then refilled and poured out again and again. We can see this process at work in the story of the Early Church as told in the Acts of the Apostles. The apostles, already filled with the Spirit at Pentecost (Acts 2:4) are filled with the Spirit again on an occasion recorded in Acts 4:31. Particularly holy, godly people are described as 'full of the Holy Spirit', Stephen, the first Christian martyr, being an example (Acts 6:5). It appears, though, that 'filling with the Spirit' is not a one-off event, but one that is repeatable, and will need to be repeated.

There also seem to have been occasions when the Holy Spirit descended on men or women and filled them for particular tasks or challenges. Peter was filled with the Holy Spirit in order to defend himself, John and the Gospel before the Jewish authorities (Acts 4:8), and we get the impression that the filling was for that one occasion. Similarly, in Acts 13:9, we find Saul being filled with the Spirit in order to denounce the sorcerer Elymas, and the form of the Greek suggests he was filled with the Spirit right then and there for that specific task. The Bible does not provide us with a name for these one-off phenomena, but it is common in certain Christian circles to describe them as 'anointings'.

They are certainly a genuine phenomenon, as the story of the Welsh preacher David Morgan, told by Dr Martyn Lloyd-Jones, bears out. One day, round about 1860, the preacher Humphrey Jones was going around Welsh chapels speaking about a revival that was taking place in the USA at that time. One of those who heard him was another preacher, by the name of David Morgan. 'I went to bed that night just David Morgan as usual,' he wrote. 'I woke up next morning like a lion, feeling that I was filled with the power of the Holy Ghost (Holy Spirit).' From then on Morgan preached with such power that people were converted in large numbers. 'But after about two years,' Morgan said, 'I went to bed one night still feeling like a lion, filled with this strange power I had enjoyed for the two years. I woke up next morning and found I had become David Morgan once more.'

There is no suggestion that Morgan had lost the Spirit's power through wrongdoing. The anointing had been given him till he completed the particular task that God had called him to. This is another way the Spirit works.

But these are all ways the Spirit tends to work. In C. S. Lewis's classic children's story, *The Lion, the Witch and the Wardrobe*, the children encounter the great and noble Lion, Aslan. Aslan represents Christ, but since God is one, what is said of him could equally well be said of the Holy Spirit. One of the other characters in the book tells the children that Aslan is not a tame lion. He is wild, but he's good. So it is with the Holy Spirit. He does not always fit very well with formality or church bureaucracy; but we need not fear him, because he is good. He is holy, after all. The only word of caution necessary is to point out that though his work is unpredictable, it will always be consistent with what the Bible says about him; and this is in fact how his work is recognised.

49 The Gifts of the Spirit
(1 Corinthians 12:1-13, 27-31)

In studying the gifts of the Spirit, we need to bear certain things in mind.

❑ We shall assume that the view that the gifts were to cease (cessationism) is unsound. The evidence for this was laid out in section 1.

❑ These gifts either cannot be exercised at all, or cannot be exercised effectively, without people being filled or anointed with the Holy Spirit (See Byway, The Holy Spirit's work).

❑ Gifts of the Spirit need to be distinguished from 'fruit of the Spirit' listed in Galatians 5:22. They differ in two ways:
• The gifts are abilities and talents. The fruit is moral qualities.
• Different people exercise different gifts of the Spirit, and nobody is expected to exercise all of them. The fruit on the other hand is for everybody all of the time.

❑ The nine gifts dealt with here are almost certainly not the only 'gifts of the Spirit'. Paul makes examples of them, it would appear, because they were the ones most involved in the problems at Corinth, but later, in 1 Corinthians 12:28, he mentions the gift of administration. Then, in the Old Testament book of Exodus, we encounter Bezalel son of Uri, who was given the task of making the Ark and the Tabernacle, because he was full of the Spirit, who had given him the gift of the most exquisite craftsmanship (Exodus 31:1-11). Some of the gifts may be already present in people before they become Christians, but they are enhanced by the Spirit; others emerge only when people have been filled with the Spirit. The latter category certainly includes prophecy and speaking in tongues, but I would not wish to commit myself about which category the other gifts would fall into.

❑ When we speak of the Spirit, the Holy Spirit is meant. We do not heal, or prophesy, or whatever, through 'the spirits of the dear departed', or through angels. In verses 4-6 Paul makes it clear, almost with vehemence, that it is the one God,

the Holy Spirit, who gives these gifts and operates through them.
❏ The gifts are not exercised separately. They do not operate very well in isolation because they need one another, and Christians, with their different gifts, complement one another and enrich one another's lives. It is also true that the boundaries between the gifts are sometimes uncertain. For instance, where prophecy ends and wisdom begins, or where healings end and miracles take over, is not always clear. But that actually does not matter too much, for the gifts are a 'package'.

Bearing all this in mind, let's move in closer and have a look in turn at each of the nine gifts Paul mentions.

Word of Wisdom

Wisdom (*sophia*) probably corresponds to the type of counsel given in the 'wisdom literature' of the Old Testament period: advice, often in easily remembered form, about how everyday life is to be lived. Such wisdom can be found in the books of Ecclesiastes and Proverbs in our Old Testament. There does also seem to have been a class of 'wise men' in Jewish society who created this body of wisdom, and so the wisdom described here is most likely to be in that same tradition. Not all wisdom is in the form of proverbs; there could be extended discourse as well.

Wisdom does appear to be a neglected gift. Recently, the 'charismatic' teacher Jack Deere has been making a plea for more wise men to be raised up in the churches, and certainly, as Agnes Sanford pointed out in her book *Healing Gifts of the Spirit*, enthusiastic Christians can often behave with a marked lack of wisdom towards one another or towards people who do not share their faith. Wisdom oils the wheels of Christian fellowship and helps us grow in maturity.

It can also contribute significantly towards 'inner healing', as in this story told by Paul Sangster of his father, the distinguished Methodist preacher W. E. Sangster:

'Jessie, a young girl in hospital, was going blind. "Mr Sangster," she said, "God is going to take my sight away." He did not answer for a little while. Then: "Don't let him, Jessie. Give it to him." "What do you mean?" "Try to pray this prayer, 'Father if for any reason I must lose my sight, help me to give it to you.'"

'She learned in time, and in due course came back to the church, where she spoke at meetings . . . .'

I should also point out, at risk of unpopularity, that the one-off, tailor-made utterances of the wise person are not termed *rhema* as opposed to *logos* which is the written word of God. By this token, pieces of wisdom would surely be *rhemata*, but Paul here speaks of the *logos sophias*. I think it important to say this, because there is teaching going around in certain Christian quarters to this effect. There is certainly an important distinction to be made between the Scriptures and the one-off utterances given by the Spirit in today's churches, but *logos* and *rhema* are not terms used to distinguish them.

Word of Knowledge

Usually, in Pentecostal and Charismatic Churches, this term is used of utterances disclosing facts about others which are supernaturally given and could not otherwise have been known by the speaker. Such utterances are very much real phenomena, and we will deal with them under prophecy, but I want to suggest humbly that they are not what is meant by 'the Word of Knowledge'. In Judaism there were wise men, teachers of the Law (otherwise known as scribes), and there were prophets. According to Paul in Ephesians 4:11, teachers were one of the foundation ministries of the Church. It would be strange if a teaching gift was not found among the gifts of the Spirit. So I want to suggest that 'word of knowledge' in all probability refers to teaching. As a piece of wisdom has it: 'All Word and no Spirit, we dry up; all Spirit and no Word, we blow up; Spirit and Word, we grow up.' Certainly, without a strong teaching ministry, there is a huge risk of Christians, captivated by the power and even the glamour of the other spiritual gifts, going off the rails.

Faith

This does not refer to the 'saving faith' which Paul mentions in Ephesians 2:8, and which all Christians need to have in order to be saved. In all probability, it means the divinely given surge of inner conviction that a specific saving, blessing or healing event is about to happen or is already happening. As these experiences of faith are borne out by events, we grow in faith, because we conclude that God, who did something remarkable once, can do it again. It was such faith that Paul and Barnabas no doubt saw in the eyes of the crippled man at Lystra (Acts 14:9).

Gifts of healings

Notice that the words here are plural. There is evidence of more than one gift of healing. There is some doubt as to whether healing miracles should be categorised under the heading of 'miracles', or under the heading of 'healings', leaving miracles to refer to other kinds of miraculous events. We do not actually know for certain. It would make life easier if we could categorise healing gifts as meaning the more natural, earthly kind of healing gifts as practised by doctors and certain kinds of complementary medicine, and since there is more than one kind of healing gift involved, perhaps we could do so. However, we must not ignore the fact that in the churches today gifted people can be found whose bodies do seem to transmit God's healing power, and the story of the healing of the woman with the haemorrhage (q.v.) indicates that Jesus' healing power could operate that way. Perhaps it is best to assume that Paul means both that kind of healing gift, and the kind practised by his 'beloved physician' Luke. Whether or not other forms of healing can be included depends very much on what form of healing we are talking about. Some complementary therapies are bogus, of limited application or dubious origin, or downright dangerous, and in our using them discernment needs to operate on a big scale. But if they are compatible with Christianity then they are gifts of God, and should be used. Remember the prophet Ezekiel's words about the leaves of the tree being for the healing of the nations.

Miraculous healings

Not all miracles are miracles of healing. Both Testaments describe remarkable events other than healings, which are often called 'nature miracles'. Writers on the subject have often categorised them separately from healing miracles, probably because they were assuming that the healings were real events which could be explained psychologically, while the nature miracles had to be legends or mistaken accounts of natural events. That distinction becomes questionable once we realise that a miraculous healing would be just as much a nature miracle as walking on water. So if it is unsound to draw a line between the gifts of miracles and healings, it is quite possible that healing miracles should come under miracles, and healing gifts refer to more natural forms of healing. The point was made above, however, that there are individuals whose bodies do seem to transmit divine healing power. As we said then, Jesus came into that category, and I'm sure that to have such a person lay hands on you must be a very different experience from having just anybody lay on hands!

The answer to all this uncertainty is surely that the boundary between healings and miracles is blurred; and it doesn't matter. It would be absurd if someone seeking healing was told, 'You're not a case for healing; we're going to send you along to our miracle worker along the corridor. You're his department.' As I have said, the gifts are a package, and they work together.

Prophecy

This gift is considered most important of all. In 1 Corinthians 14:1, Paul says we should earnestly desire the spiritual gifts, especially that we may prophesy; and in Ephesians 4:11 he says prophets are one of the foundations on which the Christian Church is built. George McLeod, founder of the Iona Community, prayed for a revival of prophecy in the Church of today, and his prayer was timely, because if we accept what Paul says, the almost complete absence of prophets and prophecies from many Christian churches today should cause us serious concern.

If she is genuine (many prophets in the past were women), she will say nothing which is incompatible with the Bible. This is one way in which we can test the reliability of the prophet's message, because prophecies do need to be tested (1 Thessalonians 5:20, 21). It is important to make this point to those who are afraid that encouraging prophecy will result in all kinds of non-Christian ideas being promoted.

Why, though, might we need further messages from God when we have the Bible? The Bible contains God's word for people everywhere, at all times. However, God often has words to say which are not for everyone, but merely for you or me at a particular point in life or a particular situation of need or opportunity. Or perhaps he may have a word for a particular church or group of people. The Bible will not tell you whether you are called to be a missionary or not: you need God's particular guidance. The Bible will not tell such-and-such a church whether or not they should start a community centre on a particular estate; here again they would need more specific guidance from God. It was apparently through prophecy that Paul and Barnabas were sent off by the church in Antioch on their first missionary journey (Acts 13:1-3). So this is the role of the prophet: not to proclaim new doctrines, but to bring God's word to particular people in particular situations.

And here is where we go and get 'words of knowledge' out

of the cupboard again, because a part of the prophetic gift is the receiving of supernatural, God-given information about people and situations. Time and again Jesus demonstrated this gift, most notably when he told the Samaritan woman at the well, whom he did not know, that she had had five husbands and was then cohabiting. Her reply was, 'Sir, I perceive that you are a prophet.' In 1 Corinthians 14:24, 25, Paul makes it clear that prophecy may disclose the secrets of a person's heart.

This has relevance to healing, for prophecy may often provide guidance to those ministering to the sufferer, or provide insights as to what to pray for, or the word of encouragement which can be very much needed and profoundly healing. Sometimes the prophet's information may be visionary. A woman with such a gift was praying with a troubled woman when she saw in her mind's eye a little toddler's shoe. She shared the picture with the other woman, who promptly burst into tears. It emerged that the woman had been ill-treated by her mother when she was small, and there had been a particularly traumatic occasion when the little girl had flushed one of her shoes down the toilet and her mother had reacted very harshly. This was a memory that needed healing.

Such instances of guidance from God, whether we call them words of knowledge or prophecies, and describe them correctly or not, are genuine phenomena. I have benefited from them myself on more than one occasion. Troubling, buried memories may need dealing with, and psychotherapy can take a long time to identify them. A gift which can go straight to the point is therefore a wonderful counselling aid.

Discernment of spirits

Messages claiming to be from God often turn out to be nothing of the kind. As chapters 2 and 3 suggest, this was an issue in the Corinthian Church. So this gift seems to have been a God-given intuition that such-and-such a message was genuinely from God or was not. It probably also had its use as an indicator of when someone was demonised. Probably it manifested itself as a deep feeling of uneasiness about a message, or a person, or, just possibly, about a place.

Speaking in tongues

This is the most controversial of the gifts. Often people find the irrational character of the gift deeply disturbing, and are inclined to regard it as pathological. It also seems novel and untried; something that mainstream denominations had apparently got on very well without for centuries. In fact it has never been completely absent from Christian experience, but it has to be admitted that it was extremely rare until the early years of the twentieth century, when it erupted in the various revivals which occurred at that time, and became a feature of the Pentecostal Churches which arose out of those revivals.

So what did Paul mean by *glossolalia*? I am speaking here mostly from pastoral experience rather than from reading. Paul speaks of 'various kinds of tongues', which alerts us to the fact that it is not a single phenomenon. There is the kind of tongue-speaking used in private prayer. There is the kind which comes to a group as an utterance from God, but which needs someone else to interpret it. Then, thirdly, and most extraordinary of all, would appear to be the kind which turns out to be an actual earthly language which the speaker has never learnt. The ability to speak other tongues symbolises the breaking down of barriers between people, represented by their different languages. It was obviously this kind of *glossolalia* that the bystanders heard spoken by the apostles when the Holy Spirit filled them at Pentecost (Acts 2:1-4). An outpouring of *glossolalia* may follow an outpouring of the Holy Spirit, and is regarded by some Christian groups as essential evidence that this has happened.

The most common use is in private prayer. But why is one's own language not enough? The gift may, arguably, have various functions. One might be that, in view of the fact that most of us run out of words when we wish to express deep emotion or talk about God, it is a blessing not to be limited in this way. Is God giving us the language in which to address him? Again, when we are too tired to frame prayers in our own language, it can be a blessing to lapse into tongues. The spirit can remain alert when the mind is tired.

A further function, and a most important one where the maintenance of mental health is concerned, could be that it is a way of painlessly talking out of our systems griefs and memories and problems which go deep and have perhaps been repressed.

Interpretation of tongues

Had Paul wished to belittle 'tongues' he would not have listed it as a gift of the Holy Spirit; neither would he have said that he thanked God that he spoke in tongues more than all of them (1 Corinthians 14:18), but when tongues were spoken in public worship he considered that they would give an unhelpful impression to visitors, or do no good to the other worshippers, unless they were exercised decently and in order, and were interpreted. Interpretation appears to have been a valuable spiritual gift in its own right.

To sum up this section, I find that each of the gifts of the Spirit seems to require one or more of the others to operate effectively; the boundaries between them are sometimes blurred; there is a package-like unity about them, and almost all of the ones Paul deals with here will at some time or other have reference to healing.

50 Anointing and the Prayer of Faith
(James 5:14-16)

We turn now to the last of the passages we shall visit, and one which is rich in insights and of great importance to the healing ministry.

The writer is not James the brother of John, who was actually one of the first Christians to be martyred, but the James who was one of the four brothers of Jesus, who became a Christian and then leader of the Jerusalem Church. His epistle, written in surprisingly elegant Greek, is much prized by Christians for its down-to-earth wisdom, which emerges particularly in these verses. The passage is again short enough to be quoted in full.

'Is any one of you sick? He should call the elders of the church to pray over him and anoint him with oil in the name of the Lord. And the prayer offered in faith will make the sick person well; the Lord will raise him up. If he has sinned, he will be forgiven. Therefore confess your sins to each other and pray for each other so that you may be healed. The prayer of a righteous man is powerful and effective.'

The first thing to note is that it is up to the sick person to send for the elders of the church. We are the ones responsible for our bodies and their care. The request also indicates a degree of faith on the sufferer's part. Francis McNutt says that prayer for healing should be offered with the sufferer only when either the patient has asked for it, or the Holy Spirit has clearly indicated it.

The elders are to be asked not only to pray for the patient, but to anoint him with oil. For centuries it was the practice of the Roman Catholic Church to anoint with oil people who were at the point of death, preparing them for what lay beyond the grave. The *Douai Version,* a Roman Catholic Bible which was translated from a Latin version of the Scriptures called the Vulgate, contained a footnote on this passage, which assumed that the passage was talking about 'Extreme Unction', as the practice is known:

'See here a plain warrant of scripture for the Sacrament of Extreme Unction, that any controversy against its institution would be against the words of the sacred text in its plainest terms.'

As a result, Protestant commentators on this passage used to work hard to explain that if you worked from the original Greek (not the Latin) this was not what it meant, and that anointing and prayer were implied for the sick, whether they were dying or not. The Greek of verse 15 actually says, 'will *save* the sick man', which could mean 'save from sin', but could also mean 'heal'; and 'sick' does not necessarily imply dying; while 'raise up' could equally as well mean 'raise from one's sick bed' as it could mean 'raise from the dead'. I say they used to work hard at this, because the Second Vatican Council, which altered Rome's position on many things, altered its attitude to anointing with oil as well. The 'Constitution on the Sacred Liturgy' (III 73ff.) specified that:

' "Extreme Unction", which may also and fittingly be called "anointing of the sick", is not a sacrament for those only who are at the point of death. Hence, as soon as any of the faithful begins to be in danger of death from sickness or old age, the appropriate time for him to receive this sacrament has already arrived.'

Anointing of the sick has always been practised in the Greek and Russian Orthodox Churches, and in recent years it has become more frequent in the new churches, and also in Anglican Churches. Morris Maddocks, a leading figure in the healing ministry in Britain, writes:

'In the Episcopal Churches, the oil of the sick, *oleum infirmorum* as it is called, is usually blessed by the bishops during the Eucharist on Maundy Thursday. More and more is this practice being revived today with the beneficial result that the ministry of healing is increasingly and rightly taking its part within the normal liturgical action of the Church.'

Maddocks also claims that anointing has often 'separated a person from his disease', giving him the power to rise above it; or has actually freed him from it.

If this is done, James promises that the prayer of faith will make the sick person well (the word used is *sozo;* literally 'save'). Note that the word he uses could mean 'save from sin', which could in this context mean preparing him for Heaven, or it could mean 'heal', because it is often used in that sense too. In the light of what we have already said, it probably means 'heal', but with overtones of salvation from sin.

So James at first sight appears to be promising that if prayer for the sick is offered, they *will* be healed, and that there is no doubt about it. But if this were true it would clash with what Paul taught regarding his thorn in the flesh, and would also tend to imply that if there was no healing it was because the sufferer or the elders lacked faith. This in turn would justify some people in the cruel practice of telling patients that if they are not healed in response to prayer then it is because they haven't enough faith.

The way out of this puzzle is to look again at the meaning of the prayer of faith. Dr Dilwyn Price, in an outstandingly helpful book on this passage called *Is any one of you sick?*, argues convincingly that faith is a God-given thing. We do not huff and puff and work up faith in ourselves: it has to come from God. So if God gives us that inner surge of conviction that our healing or someone else's healing is happening or about to happen, he does so because he intends to heal that person at that particular time.

Price also convincingly equates the prayer of faith with 'prayer in the Name', which we have already examined in the commentary on the healing of the lame man at the Temple Gate, and 'prayer in the Spirit' (Ephesians 6:18 and Jude 20). If the Spirit gives us the conviction that we must pray for a certain person for a specific healing, then we know that it is God's will to heal, and must act on the guidance. Note that there is more than one elder involved. This could well be because guidance often needs to be checked out, and if more than one person gets the same conviction, then it increases their confidence to go ahead. Where no conviction comes, they should still pray as best they can, and the experience will still be a blessing for the sufferer in one way or another.

James also promises that if the patient has sinned he will be forgiven. The word 'if' is important. No assumption is to be made that illness is a punishment for wrongdoing. It might be a *consequence* of wrongdoing, or there might be some sin that the person is guilty of but which has nothing to do with his or her illness. Then again, there may be no sin involved at all. This banishes the cruel assumption that illness is usually a punishment.

We are also commanded to confess sins, not only to God, but to one another. Confession need not be made to a priest, for James does say 'each other', and it should certainly not be a hurried, routine thing. Remember how, at the Anglican healing shrine at Walsingham, a door leads from the counselling room into the confessional, so that priest and client can move easily from one to the other. The act of confession has enormous psychological value. The sharing of a 'guilty secret', which you might have sat on for years, can be a great release.

Confession was a baby which many Protestant Churches threw out with the Roman Catholic bath water following the Reformation; with damaging effect. It is still all too common for a Christian carrying a heavy burden to find that there is no one whom he can trust sufficiently to share it with; but the value of confession and the need for it, is becoming increasingly understood once more in some Protestant churches. John Wesley's confidential 'band meetings' had verse 16 of this passage at the head of their rules. If confession is to take place, confidentiality is a 'must', as is unshockability. The confessor also needs to be a good listener. In the Old Testament, Job tells his canting, insensitive friends, 'Listen to what I am saying; that is all the comfort I ask from you' (Job 21:1, 2 in the Good News Bible). Frank Lake deemed listening to be such an important skill in the realm of healing that he devoted the first hundred pages of his huge work *Clinical Theolgy* to 'the Ministry of Listening'.

The outstanding feature of this passage is the way body, mind and spirit seem to be interlinked, and all need to be taken into consideration in the process of healing. The sick are prayed for that they might be forgiven, and sinners are prayed for that they might be healed.

section 5

Where do we go from here?

What must we do now?

What readers must now do, having stayed with this book thus far, will depend entirely on their beliefs and background, and what they hoped to learn by reading it. There could be as many courses of action as there are readers. My only hope is that having explored the New Testament with some help from this guide, they do not put the book down as if it were an airport novel, and then carry on living as if nothing had happened.

We have discovered some haunting things. Jesus of Nazareth was not a legendary figure. That is known; it isn't just an article of faith. It is also true that he changed the course of history; and that isn't something you just have to believe: it's a fact. It can also be shown beyond reasonable doubt that Jesus had a remarkable healing ministry. Again, while many of the things ascribed to him cannot be proven to be fact (as opposed to having been proved to be fiction!), there are actually many things that he can be proven beyond reasonable doubt to have done and said, and they include many of his healings and his teaching about them. True, there are many things ascribed to Jesus that he cannot be shown either to have done or not done. As a Christian I take those on trust. I believe where I cannot prove; and this is a reasonable stance when you consider how much about Jesus *can* be shown to be fact.

So non-Christians reading this book probably have a verdict to reach about Jesus, and perhaps a decision to make about him. Others who have read the book might have been believers or unbelievers who were themselves seeking healing. For them, all that we have learnt defies summary; but one can venture to hope that here or there things have been said or pointed out in the Scriptures that had God's anointing on them for them particularly, and have pointed them in the direction of healing. I suspect also that many who have stayed with the book have wanted a book that they could quarry for insights about the healing ministry, being themselves involved in such a ministry, or hoping to be. Again, there are almost as many ways ahead as there are people, but in this case I believe there are some generalisations that can be set down.

Before I do this, however, there is a question that readers may or may not have spotted, but which certainly needs answering. It goes like this: When we read about Jesus doing healings, we are surely not reading about an ordinary human being, but about someone whom Christians believe to be the Son of God. As such, did he not have powers that we can never hope to have, and doesn't that mean that we cannot use his approach to healing as a model for our own? That is a good question; but yes, I believe we can base our ministry on his, for the following reasons:

- Jesus is at times represented as teaching the disciples how to go about things, like a skilled craftsman teaching apprentices (Mark 6:6; 9:28, 29; 12:30). It is as if his teaching was designed to prepare them for future ministry along the same lines as his.
- John 14:12, while it says nothing about the 'how' of healing, nevertheless makes it abundantly clear that we can expect Christians to do similar things to Jesus.
- Jesus passed on his intimate experience of God, whereby he called him Abba (Father, or possibly Dad) (Mark 14:36), to his disciples (Matt. 6:9; Luke 11:2) and then on to the Church (Romans 8:15; Galatians 4:6).
- Jesus appears to have conferred his authority on his disciples. Matthew in particular conveys a sense of the disciples' sharing in Jesus' authority and work; while John talks of the risen Jesus meeting the disciples in the Upper Room, breathing the Holy Spirit on them, and conferring his authority on them (John 20:21-23).
- In Acts, the apostles carry out healings in the name of Jesus that are very similar to ones that he himself carried out. This is particularly true of the stories of Aeneas and Dorcas (Acts 9:32-42) (q.v.).

• Finally, there are the various word pictures used in the New Testament which seem to tie up Jesus organically with his followers. He is the Vine and they are the branches (John 15:1-7); they are like organs and limbs in his body (Romans 124-8; 1 Corinthians 12; Ephesians 4:1-13), or stones making up the walls of a spiritual house or temple in which he is the cornerstone (Ephesians 2:19-22; 1 Peter 2:4-6). All these texts make it abundantly clear that the writers of the New Testament, and Jesus himself, envisaged that Christians would carry on Christ's work in Christ's way.

Having hopefully cleared up that question, I summarise what we have learnt.

Firstly, some 'don'ts':

❏ Don't put deliverance ministry into the hands of inexperienced people.

❏ Don't be too quick to assume that sick, disturbed, or even wicked people are demonised.

❏ Don't tell sufferers whose prayers for healing have apparently gone unanswered that this is because they don't have enough faith. This is a cruel thing to do. (See the comments on James 5.)

❏ Don't belittle medicine, or encourage those apparently-healed to come off medication without checking with their doctor, or fail to advise them to have a doctor confirm their healing. Do recognise that it is more often than not God's will to heal sufferers through medicine.

Secondly, some 'do's':

❏ Be open and flexible. The way the ministry of healing is organised in one church may not be helpful in another. Special services of healing may be just the thing in one place, whereas in another, where the bulk of the congregation are not sold on the idea of healing, they may divide the church between the few zealots who are keen on healing, and the many who would rather not know about it. Some wonderful ministry can be done after morning worship in the sanctuary while the congregation adjourn to the hall or the foyer for coffee.

❏ Always accompany the healing ministry with teaching or preaching the Gospel in one form or another. This is always the way in the New Testament.

❏ Holy Communion and the gifts of the Spirit are both essential ingredients of a healing ministry. Unfortunately, Christian groups tend to lean heavily one way or the other: either towards the sacrament or towards the gifts. Both tendencies are a mistake, and we need to seek balance. John Richards speaks eloquently of the need for such a balance:

'If you will allow me to caricature Maturity and Fire when they are divorced from each other:

'*Maturity* or *Sacramentalism* divorced from Fire can lead to the occasional and well-prepared anointing of the faithful either to live or die; to meticulous documents of the Theology of healing; to the avoidance altogether of healing services because of the possible dangers; the shunning of any practice which can be abused or is not predictable. It can result in such a correctness about healing that no-one gets healed; . . .

'The *Aflame* tradition, . . . can result in a preoccupation with healing, "gazing endlessly at one's spiritual navel" as some have described it; an exclusive focus on instant cure; a glib triumphalism that has nothing of the pain or paradox of the Cross in it; an inability to cope with those whom God is leading *through* areas of hurt for healing (because it is assumed that he always leads *away* from pain); a total inability to see the healing nature of the Christian death; a lack of confidentiality; a denial of God's working in medicine, etc.'

❏ Remember the need for guidance. Where God intends to do a particular healing on a particular person at a particular time that will usually be indicated by a prophetic word, or a sense of inner conviction on the healer's part, or a surge of faith on the part of the sufferer or those who care about her.

❏ Work with the medical profession as much as you can, remembering that medicine is a wonderful gift of God. There will, sadly, be many situations, however, where no such co-operation can be arranged. It took the Piper Alpha oil-rig disaster to convince the hospital authorities in Aberdeen of how valuable the role of hospital chaplain can be; and there are areas where medical-clerical co-operation could be a lot better. Collaborate where you can, and if no such collaboration is possible, make sure that it isn't through any fault of yours. How should the healing ministry relate to the work of medicine? The sick should always be prayed *for*, and, wherever possible, prayed *with* and anointed with oil. Often we shall never know how much of a person's recovery is down to pills and how much of it is down to prayer; and it doesn't matter, for they are both gifts of God. But often, too, there will be situations where the power of medicine runs out. We are then in miracle territory, and if God's people are prayerful the guidance may well come to us that we should pray for healing against all the odds, and it happens! Chaplains and pastors also have a healing role, when, remembering the unity of body, soul and spirit, they help through conversation and prayer to put the patient in the right frame of mind for recovery, or to help the individual to live positively and victoriously with a disability, which is also a form of healing. Remember Paul's 'thorn in the flesh'.

❏ Remember, too, that the person with a healing gift is a special kind of person. One of his qualifications is usually that he is himself 'wounded'. The Jesus who healed was not a great, powerful, triumphalistic figure. He was the Suffering Servant (see section 1), who quietly and secretly walked all the way to the humiliation and brokenness of the Cross; and it was *as* such a person, not *despite* his being such a person, that he healed others. 'By his wounds we are healed' (Isaiah 53:5). Another major qualification for healers is that they are people of deep, deep spirituality. They are given to prayer and fasting and are very ready to step outside of their comfort zone in order to help others, for they have to be willing to be part of the answer to their own prayers if their prayers are to have power with God. Just as it was only through prayer and fasting (Mark 9:29) that a serious case of demonisation was dealt with, so there will be many other things, such as cancers, sexual perversions or addictions, which will not budge unless those who tackle them are very much men and women of prayer. If we want to have an effective healing ministry, and prayers that have power with God, there is a price to pay.

What must we believe?

What we believe about God – and what we believe about healing as a part of his purpose for us – is as important as what we do, because what we believe, genuinely believe, affects what we are and what we do. And just as we have learnt much from our exploration of the New Testament concerning what we should do, so we have learnt much concerning what we should believe. Hopefully, anyone reading this book as a non-Christian will have learnt enough to realise that this real historical character, Jesus of Nazareth, had a unique relationship to God, and a unique insight into what God is like and what he desires for human beings. For someone who already believes in Christ, however, what he has learnt will impact Christian beliefs in certain areas.

Whatever happened to *shalom*?

It may have puzzled readers that, having given a glowing description of *shalom* in the Introduction, I seem to have forgotten it since. This is not some sort of oversight, for a perplexing feature of the New Testament is that it really does not seem to set a lot of store by *shalom*. It is true that the word 'peace' often occurs, but when it appears it does not usually, if at all, seem to have the same meaning as *shalom*. We have seen that it often means 'inner peace', the peace that passes understanding, and it can also mean reconciliation with God and reconciliation between human beings; but it only rarely in the New Testament means the full-blooded *shalom*. No term seems to replace it, either. The Greek word for 'health', *iatrikay*, never occurs in the New Testament. What has happened?

In the New Testament the emphasis has shifted in various ways:

• The emphasis has shifted from this life to the next. In Old Testament times the belief in life after death did not burn very brightly. If, therefore, you did not achieve *shalom* in this life it was a tragedy. By contrast, the New Testament writers know that there is another life (see 1 Corinthians 15, for example), and real life, and real peace belong to that life. Not everyone is going to be blessed with health, prosperity, children and a good reputation in this life (Paul was blessed with none of them!), but that doesn't matter, because Earth is not Heaven.

• The emphasis has shifted from outside to inside. We are instead gifted with the peace that passes understanding, and one of the very reasons why it passes understanding is that it is not related to our circumstances, but comes from God. Our health is within us, and we can be fully alive, despite rotten external circumstances.

• Finally, the emphasis has shifted from us to the other person. Western individualism, coupled with an outlook which thinks relentlessly of human rights rather than of human responsibilities, means that we find it hard to grasp and live out the idea that it is the other guy who matters, not 'I'; and that Jesus matters most of all. We do seek *shalom*, but we don't seek it for ourselves; we seek it for others. William Temple once wrote that 'bread for myself is a material concern; bread for my neighbour is a spiritual concern.' We could meaningfully alter that to '*shalom* for myself is a material concern; *shalom* for my neighbour is a spiritual concern.' It is along these lines that I think we can explain the absence of *shalom* in New Testament teaching.

God may not necessarily intend *shalom* for us in this life, but he does intend something else – holiness.

Healing and Holiness

We have already noted how God's intention for his people is holiness, that they should be 'set apart' for him. What this means in practice is, firstly, a passion for right and justice in society (see for instance Isaiah 1, one of many passages in the Bible on this theme), and, secondly, a transformed character along the lines of Galatians 5:22:

'The fruit of the Spirit is love, joy, peace, patience, kindness, goodness, faithfulness, gentleness and self-control.'

It is enormously reassuring that joy and peace – inner peace – form part of the ingredients of holiness. Joy and serenity are among the most precious things in the world. They constitute inner health, and make true holiness an attractive thing, both for the holy person herself and those who witness her conduct and attitude.

Healing is the handmaid of holiness. It is not the same thing as holiness, but makes it possible for holiness to achieve its purposes by helping to create a fit body with which to serve God, to minister *shalom* to others, and also to bring about inner healing, thereby setting people free to be holy. Often, to be holy you need to be whole. The process of healing is therefore part of the Kingdom of God at work. This brings us to the next thing.

Kingdom

Jesus' teaching really had only one theme: the Kingdom of God, or, to translate it more accurately, the *Kingship* of God. Theologians offer many different definitions of the Kingdom, but the one I find most helpful is that of Norman Perrin:

'The Kingdom of God is the power of God expressed in deeds. It is that which God does wherein it becomes apparent that God is King.'

Healings and other miracles are obvious examples of God's Kingdom at work. Remember the words of Jesus: 'If I drive out demons by the Spirit of God, then the kingdom of God has come upon you' (Matthew 12:28). But those words indicate that there is an opposing kingdom of evil which Jesus had come to defeat: the kingdom of Satan. So we find an element of conflict in Jesus' mission both then and now. Jesus was manifested that he might 'destroy the devil's work' (1 John 3:8). You could say that he defeated error in his teachings, defeated sin on the Cross, defeated death through his rising from the dead, and defeated sickness, which is part of the kingdom of evil, through his healing power.

Now the power of the Kingdom of God is already at work, but the Kingdom of God has not yet fully arrived. Christ will come again, and then the Kingdom will have fully come. Sometimes I have found myself driving across the vast landscape of Northumberland on a cloudy day. On some such days there will in places be breaks in the cloud, and shafts of sunlight will break through the gloom, lighting up a farm here, a field or a cottage there. One day, all the clouds will surely roll away, and everything will be bathed in light; but for the time being the light illuminates things here and there. Much of the world is still in gloom, but the Kingdom of God is around, and brings light and life, like shafts of sunlight, into this church, that person's life, or the life of that community or that country. And often it does so in the form of healing.

Cross

We think, finally, of the great event that made all this possible. The central teaching of Christianity, following the New Testament, is that by dying upon the Cross Jesus, the 'Suffering Servant', broke down the barrier of guilt that separated humanity from God, and made it possible for God's power and love to flow through to us. 'With his wounds we are healed.'

So we end our journey in Jerusalem. There, two possible sites of Calvary, the hillock where Jesus was crucified, are shown to the tourist. One of them is the Church of the Holy

Sepulchre, crowded with pilgrims, its dark interior stuffed with candles and icons. The other place lies a few hundred metres to the north, outside the city wall, and is known as The Garden Tomb. It may not be the site of Calvary, but with its shady olive trees, and authentic tombs carved out of the rock, it looks far more like the site of his crucifixion and burial than the church does. It is a beautiful spot. One of the most haunting aspects of the place is that your walk through the garden ends at the hillock which is reputed to be the site of Calvary, and as you look down, you see, at the foot of Calvary, a bus station! Buses depart from there (or used to) for towns all over the West Bank Territories.

For me this symbolises a lot of things. It symbolises how, when Jesus took up his mission, he, as it were, got on a bus from which he could often have alighted (for instance in the Garden of Gethsemane) before he reached the terminus at Calvary; but he never did. He went all the way to the Cross so that all humanity, including the readers of this book, might become fully human and fully alive. It also says to me that all roads to life start at the Cross. This seems a suitable spot to end our 'tour', which I hope has turned into a pilgrimage.

Soli Deo Gloria.

APPENDIX
Other Gospel Passages on Healing

This guide has examined the most important passages on healing in the New Testament, together with all the healing stories, but there are many other passages on the subject in the gospels which would repay study, preferably with the aid of a popular commentary on the book concerned.

We present now two lists of passages. The first is a list of 'summary statements' in Matthew, Mark and Luke. These are not healing stories as such, but little passages which depict Jesus carrying out healings on a big scale. The second is a list of the other relevant passages. As with the arrangement of the healing stories, both lists begin with the passages which are to be found in Mark and in the two other gospels, then those in Matthew and Luke but not in Mark, then those in one gospel only. There are no John passages listed among the summary statements because there are no such statements in John's gospel.

Summary Statements

1. Mark 1:32-34	Matthew 8:16, 17	Luke 4:40, 41
2. Mark 1:39	Matthew 4:23-25	Luke 6:17-19
3. Mark 3:10,11	Matthew 12:15,16	
4. Mark 6:5, 6	Matthew 13:58	
5. Mark 6:53-56	Matthew 14:34-36	Mark 13:58
6.	Matthew 11:4, 5	Luke 7:21, 22
7.	Matthew 14:14	Luke 19:11
8.	Matthew 9:35	
9.	Matthew 15:29-31	
10.	Matthew 19:2, 11-13	
11.	Matthew 21:14	
12.		Luke 5:15
13.		Luke 13:32

Note that Matthew has twice as many summary statements as either of the other two, suggesting that his habit of making long stories short is not an attempt to play down the miraculous.

Other Passages
1. Mark 2:17; Matthew 9:12; Luke 5:31f ('It is not the healthy who need a doctor, but the sick.'
2. Mark 3:22-27; Matthew 12:25-29; Luke 11:17-22 (Beelzebub controversy).
3. Mark 6:7; Matthew 10:1; Luke 4:33-37 (Authority over evil spirits).
4. Mark 6:12, 13; Luke 9:1-6 (Summary of the disciples' healing activity).
5. Mark 8:11, 12; Matthew 16:1-4 (No sign shall be given).
6. Mark 9:38-41; Luke 9:49, 50 ('We saw a man driving out demons in your name').
7. Mark 11:20-24; Matthew 21:19-22 (Withered fig tree).
8. Mark 15:29-31; Matthew 27:39-43; Luke 23:35 ('He saved others; he cannot save himself').
9. Matthew 4:5, 6; Luke 4:9, 10 (Temptations).
10. Matthew 7:15-20; Luke 6:43, 44 (Tree known by its fruits).
11. Matthew 11:2-6; Luke 7:18-23 (The Baptist's question).
12. Matthew 11:20-24; Luke 10:13-15 (Woe on unrepentant cities where healings had been done).
13. Matthew 12:39-41; Luke 11:29-31 (The sign of Jonah).
14. Matthew 12:43-45; Luke 11:24-26 (The homeless demon).
15. Matthew 7:21-23 ('I never knew you').
16. Matthew 10:5-8 (Freely you have received, freely give)
17. Matthew 11:28-30 (Comfort for the heavy-laden).
18. Matthew 18:18 (Binding and loosing).
19. Matthew 18:19, 20 (Two or three need to agree).
20. Luke 1:39-45 (The baby leaping in its mother's womb suggests effect on children of pre-natal events).
21. Luke 13:1-5 (Relationship between sin and catastrophe).
22. John 1:45-51 (Jesus has supernatural knowledge about Nathaniel).

23. John 2:18-23 (Signs are asked of Jesus to show his authority).
24. John 3:1-3 ('No-one could perform the miraculous signs you are doing if God were not with him').
25. John 6:28-33 (True bread from heaven).
26. John 7:1-5 (Jesus' brothers suggest he goes to Jerusalem and performs signs).
27. John 7:31 ('When the Christ comes, will he do more miraculous signs than this man?')
28. John 10:22-42 (The unbelief of the Jews).
29. John 12:37-41 (Blindness of spirit leads to unbelief).
23. John 14:12 (Believers will do greater works than Jesus).
31. John 15:25 (Miracles can be met with hatred).

Bibliography

Aune, D. E., The Apocalypse of John and Graeco-Roman Revelatory Magic (in *New Testament Studies* vol. 33).
Baker, Roger, *Binding the Devil: Exorcism Past and Present* (London 1974).
Barrett, C. K., *I Corinthians* (London 1968).
Barrett, C. K., *II Corinthians* (London 1972).
Barrett, C. K. *The Gospel of John* (London 1982).
Barth, Karl, *Epistle to the Philippians* (Eng. Edn. London 1962).
Bede, *A History of the English Church and People* (Harmondsworth 1955).
Bishop of Exeter's Commission on Exorcism. Report (London 1972).
Bock, Darrell L., *The NIV Application Commentary: Luke* (Grand Rapids 1976).
Boggs, Wade, *Faith Healing and the Christian Faith* (Richmond Virginia, 1956).
Booth, Howard, *Healing is Wholeness* (London 1987).
Bruce, F. F., *The Book of the Acts* (London 1965).
Bruce, F. F., *Commentary on the Book of Acts* (London 1954).
Buckley, Michael, *Christian Healing: a Catholic Approach to God's Healing Love* (London 1990).
Buckley, Michael, *His Healing Touch* (London 1987).
Bultmann, Rudolph, *History of the Synoptic Tradition* (ET 2nd. Edn. Oxford 1968).
Bultmann, Rudolph, *Theology of the New Testament* vol.1 (ET London 1952).
Caird, G. B., *Pelican Gospel Commentary: St. Luke* (Harmondsworth, 1963).
Carson, D. A., *Showing the Spirit.* (Grand Rapids 1987).
Chavda, Mahesh, *Only Love can make a Miracle* (Ann Arbor 1990).
Cole, Alan, *Tyndale New Testament Commentary: Galatians* (Leicester 1974).
Collins, Gary R., *Christian Counselling* (Waco Texas 1980).

Cullmann, O., *Christianity Divided* (London 1962).
Dale, David, *In His Hands: Towards a Theology of Healing* (London 1989).
Dickinson, Robert, *God does Heal Today* (Edinburgh 1995).
Douglas. J. D. (ed.) *The Illustrated Bible Dictionary* (Leicester 1980).
Dunn, James D. G., *Jesus and the Spirit* (London 1975).
Dunn, James D. G., *Epworth Commentaries: The Acts of the Apostles* (Peterborough 1996).
Dunn, James D. G., *Jesus Remembered* (Grand Rapids 2003).
Edmunds and Scorer, *Some Thoughts on Faith Healing* (London 1979).
Enoch, M. David, *Healing the Hurt Mind* (London 1983).
English, Donald, *The Message of Mark* (Leicester 1992).
Farrer, F. W., *The Life and Work of St. Paul* (London 1989).
Fernando, Ajith, *NIV Application Commentary: Acts* (Grand Rapids 1998).
Finlay, Ian, *Columba* (London 1979).
Fleischmann, Paul R., *The Healing Spirit* (London 1990).
Foakes-Jackson, F. A., and Kirsopp Lake, *The Beginnings of Christianity Part I* vol.ii (London 1922).
Fridrichsen, Anton: *The Problem of Miracles in the New Testament* (ET Minneapolis 1972).
Fuller, R. H., *Interpreting the Miracles* (London 1963).
Gardner, R. F. R., *A Doctor investigates Healing Miracles* (London 1986).
Garrett, Susan R., *The Demise of the Devil: Magic and the Demonic in Luke's Writings* (Minneapolis 1989).
Goleman, Daniel, *Emotional Intelligence* (English edn. London 1995).
Goulder, Michael, *Midrash and Lection in Matthew* (London 1974).
Green, E. M. B., *The Meaning of Salvation* (London 1962).
Green, Michael, *The Message of Matthew* (Leicester 2000).
Guidelines for Good Practice for Those involved in the Healing Ministry (Methodist Leaflet).

Haenchen, Ernst, *The Acts of the Apostles* (ET Oxford 1971).
Harper, Michael, *Spiritual Warfare* (London 1970).
Hendrickson, William, *The Gospel of Matthew* (Edinburgh 1974).
Hering, Jean, *The First Epistle of S. Paul to the Corinthians* (ET London 1962).
Hollenweger, Walter, *The Pentecostals* (ET London 1962).
Holmes, Michael W., *NIV Application Commentary: I & II Thessalonians* (Grand Rapids 1998).
House of Bishops' Working Party, *A Time to Heal: the Development of Good Practice in the Healing Ministry.*
Huck, Albert, *Synopsis of the First Three Gospels* (Revised edn. Oxford 1963).
Huggett, John and Christine, *It Hurts to Heal* (Eastbourne 1984).
Huggett, Joyce, *Listening to God* (London 1986).
Huggett, Joyce, *Listening to Others* (London 1988).
Huggett, Joyce, *Open to God* (London 1986).
Hunter, A. M., *According to John* (London 1968).
In Search of Health and Wholeness (Methodist Division of Social Responsibility Workbook, London 1985).
Inwood, Richard, *Biblical Perspectives on Counselling* (Bramcote, Notts. 1980).
Irvine, Doreen, *From Witchcraft to Christ* (London 1973).
Jefferies, Esmond, *The Power and the Glory* (London 1991).
Jeremias, Joachim, *New Testament Theology* vol.1 (London 1971).
Johnson, Paul, *A History of Christianity* (London 1976).
Kelsey, Morton, *Healing and Christianity* (New York 1973).
Kelsey, Morton, *Speaking with Tongues* (London 1970).
Kummel, W. G., *Promise and Fulfilment* (ET 2nd edn. London 1961).
Lake, Frank, *Clinical Theology* Abr. Martin H. Yeomans. (London 1986).
Lake, Frank, *The Dynamic Cycle: Introduction to the Model* (Nottingham 1986).

Lambourne, R. A., *The Deliverance Map of Disease and Sin* (1974 Article in 'Contact' no. 4).
Lambourne, R. A., *Wholeness, Community and Worship* (1974 article in 'Contact').
Latourelle, Rene, *The Miracles of Jesus and the Theology of Miracles* (ET Mahwah NJ. Originally publ. in French 1988).
Lawrence, Peter H., *The Hot Line* (Eastbourne 1990).
Lewis, David, *Healing: Faith, Fantasy or Fact?* (London 1989).
Lewis, C. S., *The Lion, the Witch and the Wardrobe* (pb. London 1983).
Lewis, C. S., *Miracles: A Preliminary Study* (London 1947).
Lowe, Chuck, *Territorial Spirits and World Evangelisation* (Fearn, Ross-Shire 1998).
Maddocks, Morris, *Journey to Wholeness* (London 1986).
Maddocks, Morris, *The Christian Healing Ministry* (London 1981).
Manson, T. W, *The Sayings of Jesus* (London 1949).
Martin, R. P., *The Epistle of Paul to the Philippians* (2nd Edn. Leicester 1987).
McAll, Kenneth, *Healing the Family Tree* (London 1982).
McManus, Jim, *Healing in the Spirit* (Chawton, Hants. 2002).
McNeile, A. H., *The Gospel according to St Matthew* (London 1961).
McNutt, Francis, *The Power to Heal* (Notre Dame, Indiana 1977).
McNutt, Francis, *Healing* (Notre Dame, Indiana 1974).
Methodist Statement on the Church and the Ministry of Healing, adopted by the Methodist Conference 1977.
Mitton, C. L. *The Epistle of James* (London 1966).
Morris, Leon, *Tyndale New Testament Commentary: Luke* (Leicester 1974).
Morris, Leon, *Tyndale New Testament Commentary: I & II Thessalonians* (Leicester 1956).
Motyer, Alec, *The Prophecy of Isaiah* (Leicester 1993).
Newbigin, Leslie, *The Light has Come: An Exposition of the Fourth Gospel* (Grand Rapids 1983).
Newton, John A., *The Fruit of the Spirit in the Lives of Great*

Christians (London 1979).
Nouwen, Henri, *The Wounded Healer* (London 1994).
Pain, Tim, *Deliverance* (Ashburnham Insights Book, Eastbourne 1987).
Pain, Tim, *Counselling* (Ashburnham Insights Book, Eastbourne 1987).
Pain, Tim, *Blessing and Cursing* (Ashburnham Insights Book, Eastbourne 1987).
Pain, Tim, *Intercession* (Ashburnham Insights Book, Eastbourne 1987).
Price, Dilwyn, *Is any one of you Sick?* (Fearn, Ross-shire, 1997).
Peddie, J. Cameron, *The Forgotten Talent* (London 1961).
Perrin, Norman: *Rediscovering the Teaching of Jesus* (London 1967).
Peters, John; Frank Lake, *The Man and His Work* (London 1989).
Peterson, Robert, *Roaring Lion* (London 1968).
Porter, Roy, *The Greatest Benefit to Mankind: A Medical History of Humanity from Antiquity to the Present* (London 1997).
Powell, Graham and Shirley, *Christian Set Yourself Free* (Chichester 1983).
Pytches, David, *Come, Holy Spirit* (London 1985).
Pytches, David, *Does God Speak Today?* (London 1989).
Rawlinson, A. E. J., *St Mark* (London 1925).
Rees-Larcombe, Jennifer, *Unexpected Healing* (London 1991).
Richards, John, (abr.) *Report of 1958 Archbishops' Commission on Healing* (London 1986).
Richards, John, *But Deliver us from Evil: an Introduction to the Demonic in Pastoral Care* (London 1974).
Richards, John, *The Church's Healing Ministry* (Paper read at United Reformed Church's National Conf. on Health and healing, 1981).
Richards, John, *The Question of Healing Services* (London 1989).

Richardson, Alan, *The Miracle-Stories of the Gospels* (London 1941).
Robertson, Edwin, *The Biblical Bases of Healing* (Evesham 1988).
Sanders, J. N. & Mastin, B.A. *A Commentary on the Gospel According to St John* (London 1968).
Sandford, John and Paula, *Healing the Wounded Spirit* (Tulsa 1985).
Sandford, John and Paula, *The Transformation of the Inner Man* (Tulsa 1982).
Sandford, Paula, *Healing Victims of Sexual Abuse* (Tulsa 1988).
Sanford, Agnes, *The Healing Light* (Evesham 1949).
Sanford, Agnes, *Healing Gifts of the Spirit* (Evesham 1966).
Sanford, Agnes, *Sealed Orders* (Plainfield NJ 1972).
Sangster, Paul, *Dr Sangster* (London 1962).
Sheils W. J. (ed.), *Studies in Church History* vol.19 'The Church and Healing' (Oxford 1982).
Smail, Tom, *Reflected Glory* (London 1975).
Smith Fred, *God's Gift of Healing* (Chichester 1986).
Stapleton, Ruth Carter, *The Experience of Inner Healing* (Texas 1976).
Stapleton, Ruth Carter, *The Gift of Inner Healing* (Texas 1976).
Stevenson J., *A New Eusebius* (London 1960).
Tasker, R. V. G., *Tyndale New Testament Commentary: James* (Leicester 1955).
Tate, Tim, *Children for the Devil* (London 1991).
Taylor, John V., *Enough is Enough* (London 1973).
Taylor, Vincent, *The Gospel of Saint Mark* (London 1952).
Temple, William, *Readings in St John's Gospel* (London 1939).
Theissen, Gerd, *Miracle-Stories of the Early Christian Tradition* (ET Edinburgh 1983, Original German 1974).
Thielman, Frank, *NIV Application Commentary: Philippians (Grand Rapids* 1998).
Thomas, John Christopher, *The Devil, Disease and Deliverance: Origins of Illness in New Testament Thought* (Sheffield 1998).
Thurian, Max, (ed.) *Ecumenical Perspectives on Baptism,*

Eucharist and Ministry (World Council of Churches Faith and Order Paper 116 [Geneva 1983]).
Urquhart, Colin, *Anything You Ask* (London 1979).
Van der Loos, H., *The Miracles of Jesus* (Leiden 1965).
Virgo (ed.), *First Aid in Pastoral Care* (Edinburgh 1987).
Von Rad, Gerhard, *Wisdom in Israel* (English edn. London 1972).
Wagner and Pennoyer (eds.), *Wrestling with Dark Angels* (Eastbourne 1990).
Ward, Neville, *The Use of Praying* (London 1967).
Warfield, B. B., *Counterfeit Miracles* (Edinburgh 1972). (First publ. America 1918 as *Miracles Yesterday and Today: True or False?*)
Wilkinson, John, *Health and Healing: Studies in New Testament Faith and Practice* (Edinburgh 1980).
Wilson, Leonard C., *The Kingdom and the Principalities: Real and Counterfeit Healing* (Undated Crowhurst Original Paper).
Wimber, Carol, *John Wimber: the Way it Was* (London 1999).
Wimber, John, *Power Evangelism* (British edn. London 1985).
Wimber, John, *Power Healing* (London 1986).
Witherington III, Ben, *Conflict and Community in Corinth: a Socio-rhetorical Commentary on I and II Corinthians* (Grand Rapids 1995).
Wright, N. T., *Matthew for Everyone* (London 2002, and other titles in same series).
Yonggi-Cho, Paul, *The Fourth Dimension* (South Plainfield NJ 1979).